His Majesty's Theatre

One Hundred Years of Glorious Damnation

Edi Swan

Black & White Publishing

First published 2006
by Black & White Publishing Ltd,
99 Giles Street, Edinburgh EH6 6BZ

ISBN -13 978 184502 102 3
ISBN -10 1 84502 102 9

British Library Cataloguing in publication data: a catalogue record for
this book is available from The British Library

Designed by Creative Link, North Berwick
www.creativelink.tv

Printed and bound in Poland
www.polskabook.pl

Dedicated to the memory of
Dean Campbell Adamson
1921–83,
Chaplain to His Majesty's Theatre,
whose unpublished manuscript,
A Theatre and a City,
provided the inspiration and foundation
for this book.

Acknowledgements

The author also wishes to acknowledge the invaluable assistance of the following contributors: Jim Pratt, former Senior Librarian, Aberdeen Central Library for access to his vast collection of theatre memorabilia; Catherine Taylor of the Local Studies Department at Aberdeen Central Library for assistance in researching material; James and Anne Donald for the use of their memories and access to their scrapbook; Peter Donald for help with family photographs; Gary Swan for invaluable help with computer technology; Sonja Rasmussen for time-consuming editorial guidance; Duncan Hendry and all the staff at His Majesty's Theatre, who suffered with a smile the many requests for assistance; and the following, who gave of their time to supply valuable and interesting material: Norman Adams, Mike Dey, Karen Dinardo, Buff Hardie, Honor Inglis, David Marshall, Stephen Robertson, Trevor Smith, Duncan Smith and David Steel.

Thanks also to following theatre critics whose penmanship over the years has provided informative and enjoyable reading: G. R. Harvey, Angus McPhail, George Fraser, Jack Scott, Alastair Selway and Roddy Phillips.

My appreciation also goes to my copy-editor, Andrew Burnet, and the staff of Black & White Publishing.

And a final thanks to Sheila who was always confident that this book should and could be written.

The new extension

The refurbished Stalls Bar

BAGSHOT PARK

His Majesty's Theatre has been at the centre of the performing arts in Aberdeen since it was built in 1906 and the Theatre's Centenary is the most significant milestone in the history of this iconic building. It is quite remarkable that a building designed over 100 years ago is still delivering performances of the highest quality to over 200,000 customers each year.

Of course the theatre has had to reinvent itself over the years with major refurbishments in the 1930's, 1980's and most recently in 2005 when the most extensive redevelopment in its history was completed. The theatre is now well placed to deliver performances well into its second century.

This book tells the story of theatres in Aberdeen from the early part of the 20th Century and sets the context for the story of His Majesty's. It also describes the many reincarnations of the building and the fascinating characters who have been involved with His Majesty's over the years. The author, Edi Swan, is the leading authority on the history of HMT and has a wealth of anecdotes which I am sure will inform and entertain the reader.

I hope you will enjoy this celebration of His Majesty's Theatre and wish everyone involved at HMT good luck in the centenary year and beyond.

Edward

HRH The Earl of Wessex KCVO

Sitting at the
head of a garden

Contents

William Wallace shows the way to education, salvation and damnation

The Prologue

Education, Salvation and Damnation

I thought it would be helpful to explain the reason for the title of this book. Mention the phrase 'education, salvation and damnation' to any true Aberdonian and they will immediately identify it with the three superbly elegant buildings sitting on Rosemount Viaduct – The Public Library, The South United Church (now St Mark's) and His Majesty's Theatre. There was also a 'transportation' – Schoolhill Railway Station – but that has long since disappeared into the mists of time.

Citizens of Aberdeen have long been famous for poking fun at themselves – Union Street deserted on a flag day and crowded on a house-to-house collection – so, when Robert Arthur claimed, on the opening night of His Majesty's on Monday, 3 December 1906, that his new theatre would admirably complement its neighbours, he was asking to be challenged and within days the joke was born.

'Damnation' it might be but His Majesty's Theatre represented, at that time, the pinnacle of theatrical development in the city – a development that began in an open field then progressed through timber and canvas pavilions, stone and lime to become the building we know and love. A superb example of classical Ionic architecture, built in sparkling granite from Kemnay and Tillyfourie and placed at the head of a beautiful sunken garden, if His Majesty's is a damnation – as some might still suggest – then it is a glorious one.

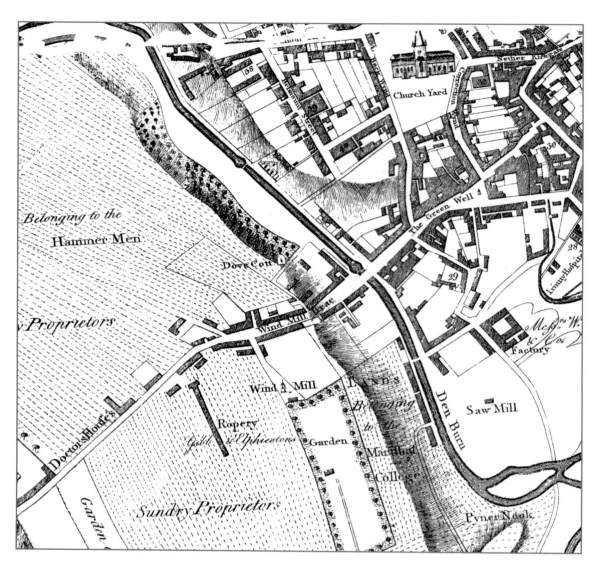

Above: Alexander Milne's Map 1789

Right: Well o' Spa

The Overture

The Early Years of Theatrical Entertainment in the City of Aberdeen

Playfields and the Early Theatres

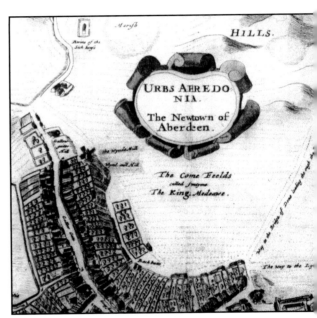

Parson Gordon's Map 1661

It is perhaps appropriate that His Majesty's should sit next to a church. The earliest theatrical performance recorded in Scotland came about because of a need to teach and preach a religious message. Around 1440, Aberdeen Town Council commissioned the Abbot of Bon Accord, assisted by his prior, to present the play *Halyblude* two weeks before the festival of Corpus Christi. The abbot and prior were not religious officials but young men appointed by the Council to ensure that religious festivals were properly observed and presented. They completely fulfilled their duties on 13 May 1440, on the 'Playfield of Wyndmylhill', and were duly paid the fee of £8 6s 8d Scots under a Municipal Statute of 5 September 1442. This is the earliest record in Scotland of a professional theatrical performance.

There are a few contenders for the site of the Playfield. Parson James Gordon's map of 1661 shows a Windmill Hill at the top of the Gallowgate, while Council records show a Playfield near the Spa Well, which was leased, on 13 May 1635, to the artist George Jamesone. But the most popular assumption is that it was to the

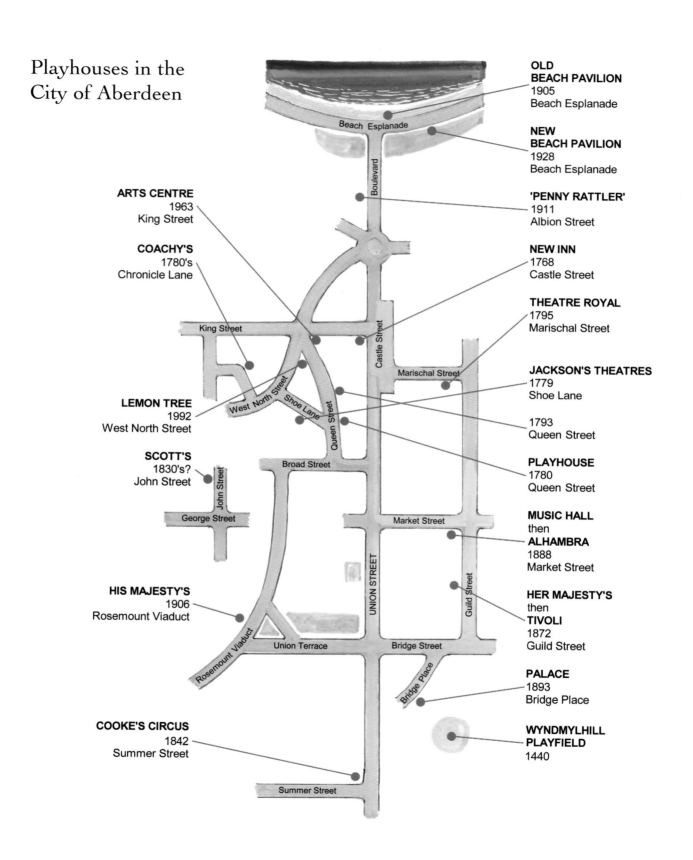

Playhouses in the
City of Aberdeen

OLD
BEACH PAVILION
1905
Beach Esplanade

NEW
BEACH PAVILION
1928
Beach Esplanade

'PENNY RATTLER'
1911
Albion Street

ARTS CENTRE
1963
King Street

COACHY'S
1780's
Chronicle Lane

NEW INN
1768
Castle Street

THEATRE ROYAL
1795
Marischal Street

JACKSON'S THEATRES
1779
Shoe Lane

LEMON TREE
1992
West North Street

1793
Queen Street

SCOTT'S
1830's?
John Street

PLAYHOUSE
1780
Queen Street

MUSIC HALL
then
ALHAMBRA
1888
Market Street

HIS MAJESTY'S
1906
Rosemount Viaduct

HER MAJESTY'S
then
TIVOLI
1872
Guild Street

PALACE
1893
Bridge Place

COOKE'S CIRCUS
1842
Summer Street

WYNDMYLHILL
PLAYFIELD
1440

Beach Esplanade

Boulevard

King Street

Castle Street

Marischal Street

West North Street

Shoe Lane

Queen Street

Broad Street

John Street

George Street

Market Street

Guild Street

UNION STREET

Rosemount Viaduct

Union Terrace

Bridge Street

Bridge Place

Summer Street

William
Shakespeare

south of the town, in the area, shown in Alexander Milne's map of
1789, bounded by Windmill Brae and below Crown Street. It is
difficult to make a positive identification since there are no records of
windmills in the city before 1609.

Religious pageants continued in later years under the auspices of
the trade guilds though they did not always prove reliable. In 1924,
while researching her thesis *Mediaeval Plays in Scotland*, Anna Jean Mill MA
discovered that in 1532 the Baxters (bakers) Guild were fined for failing in
their duties, the Listers (dyers) and Barbers in 1533 and again the Listers in 1539.

Theatre, as we define it today, only came about in 1601 when King James VI
invited his kinswoman Queen Elizabeth to send a company of comedians to
Scotland. After a successful run in Edinburgh, they duly arrived in Aberdeen and
so pleased the magistrates of the city that not only did they receive thirty-two
merks but also the freedom of the city. This was bestowed on Lawrence Fletcher
and his company on 9 October of that year. Legend would have it that the great
playwright William Shakespeare was present on that occasion. Unfortunately, the
record of the Freedom Ceremony does not list the names of the members of the
company but historical accounts reveal that Fletcher and Shakespeare did not link
up until 1603.

There are no records of plays being performed in the city for the next 150 years.
This was an inactive period for drama in Scotland – partly due to the Civil War and
the suppression of theatre that followed but also thanks to the Jacobite uprisings.
The city fathers also harboured the suspicion that strolling players lacked the moral
fibre expected of visiting tourists. An Edinburgh company attempted a visit in 1745
but was banned by local ministers and magistrates. They returned in 1751 and set
up their booth in the Spital, outside the city boundary, but departed fairly quickly,
disappointed and penniless.

Theatre Lane down by the
harbour – a lingering memory
of the Theatre Royal

A great leap forward came in 1768, when
William Fisher set up a theatre in a hall in
the New Inn, an upmarket hostelry in the
Castlegate, on the corner of Union Street and King Street, later to become a bank
and now a restaurant. Among the company of players was the young actor William
Woodfall, who switched careers from journalism to acting and back again. He later
moved to London where, with a fellow actor named James Perry as his editor, he
founded *The Morning Chronicle*, which carried the first verbatim reports of debates in
the Houses of Parliament.

Next on the scene are two small theatres erected by one John Jackson, formerly
the manager of the Theatre Royal in Edinburgh. The first of these opened in Shoe
Lane in 1779; the second in Queen Street, in 1793, coinciding with the publication
of Jackson's book, *The History of the Scottish Stage*. Sadly few records exist of these
ventures but we do know that the leading man in Shoe Lane was the actor West
Digges, a box-office hero famous for his roles as Macbeth and as Wolsey in
Shakespeare's Henry VIII. A protégé of the Irish playwright and politician Richard
Brinsley Sheridan, he toured successfully throughout the country, married the

famous but strangely named Irish actress George Anne Bellamy and died in 1786 in Cork, where he is buried in the Cathedral.

A splendid little theatre had a brief life in an inn behind Queen Street, from 1780 until 1789. The Playhouse was noted for a character called Mad Sinclair, an eccentric schoolmaster who, from a special chair in the second row of benches in the gallery, conducted the applause or hisses and boos from the 'gods'. Religious opposition to the stage in Aberdeen enjoyed a resounding victory when the Playhouse was converted into a chapel, where the Rev. Charles Chandler combined the preaching of the gospel with teaching English to ladies and gentlemen. However, the balance was

sustained – a church at the foot of Market Street had been converted into Macfarland's Music Hall.

A rival playhouse at this time was Coachy's Playhouse in Chronicle Lane, just off Queen Street. It was so named because its proprietor was a well-known local coachman. It was managed by a Mr Sutherland, whose ambitions far outweighed his business acumen and he ended up in financial ruin. This theatre is noted for the introduction of boxes and a 'starring' policy. In earlier theatres, all roles were played by members of the resident company. By contrast, Coachy's Playhouse highlighted well-known actors and actresses in their famous roles – a practice still favoured by modern commercial theatres.

The former
Theatre Royal
on Marishal
Street

The Real Theatres

The Theatre Royal

The definition of a 'real' theatre encompasses seats in the stalls, a circle and boxes for the richer patrons so that they can be envied by lesser mortals, a gallery with benches for the rowdier elements, suitable decor to enhance the performance, a proper stage, staging equipment and a range of dressing rooms. The first in Aberdeen to fit this bill came in 1795 with the opening of the Theatre Royal in Marischal Street.

Its birth was not an easy one. Building commenced in 1789, under the instruction of John Jackson, actor, dramatist and manager, who had dreams of running theatres in all the major Scottish cities – dreams that ended with his bankruptcy. After sitting half-built for six years, the Theatre Royal was rescued and completed by Stephen Kemple, brother of the noted actress Mrs Sarah Siddons. The rescue was achieved through a process that foreshadows financial practice in today's theatres. Kemple put together a syndicate of twenty-four investors, each of whom contributed £25 in return for five per cent of the takings, a heritable security on the building and a free ticket for every performance. He also supplied the timber for the roof, which he bought from a circus in Edinburgh for £300. The arrangement did not bring great riches to Kemple and, within a short time, he relinquished his interest.

Ensuing managers were noted only for their inability to pay the rent. In 1811, total closure threatened and a sale by roup was only avoided when John Fraser took over the lease. He was succeeded in 1814 by Corbett Ryder, who ran the theatre with great panache and success until his death in 1842. He brought great names to Aberdeen – Edmund Kean, Helen Faucit and William Charles Macready. During his visits, Macready fell in love with and married Katherine Atkins, daughter of the theatre's scenic artist.

Ryder's widow, the actress Jessie Fraser, married John Pollock, an actor in the company, and they continued to run the Theatre Royal until his death in 1854 and the management passed to his two sons-in-law. Having served the city well, the Royal was faced with opposition from the new Theatre and Opera House on Guild Street and closed its doors. In 1875, the building was sold for £1,160, less than half its original cost, to the Church of Scotland. Today it is the Elim Pentecostal Church, its former life identified only by Theatre Lane at the harbour's edge.

This is the Tivoli (Her Majesty's Theatre and Opera House)

Her Majesty's Theatre and Opera House

In the late 1800s, theatrical performances had become respectable. Touring productions were bringing well-known shows and stars out into the provinces and this signalled the end of local 'stock' companies. A group of influential citizens felt the need to enhance cultural enlightenment in the city and, in particular, to bring grand opera within its boundaries.

James Rhind Gibson

The Aberdeen Theatre and Opera House Company included: Newell Burnett, advocate, of Kyllachie; John Gray Chalmers, publisher of the *Aberdeen Journal*; Alexander Milne Ogston of Ardoe; John Moir Clark of Garthdee House; William Duthie, shipowner, of Cairnbulg; John Willet, civil engineer; William Stevenson, merchant, of Viewfield; John Gordon of Craigmyle; and George Washington Wilson, artist and photographer. Supported by a loan of £3,000 from the Northern Assurance Company, they built Her Majesty's Theatre and Opera House on a site in Guild Street owned partly by Stevenson and Washington Wilson. Designed by the most prestigious theatre architect of the day, C. J. Phipps, it opened on 19 December 1872 at a cost of £8,400 and seated 1,650 patrons. It was named in honour of Queen Victoria, who was by then a frequent and popular visitor to Balmoral Castle in Aberdeenshire.

Under the inspired management of William Gomersal, himself the son of an acclaimed actor at the Theatre Royal, Her Majesty's enjoyed great success. The opening performance of *The Lady of Lyons* featured a great star of the London stage, James Rhind Gibson, an Aberdonian born and bred.

Her Majesty's Opera House opening night banner

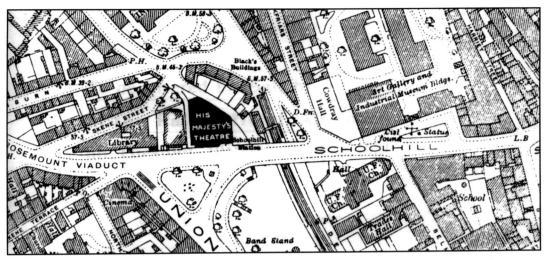

A map showing the spot that was chosen for the location of the new His Majesty's Theatre

After Gomersal's departure down south in June 1880, the theatre went into a slight decline until it was rescued by William McFarland of Dundee who ran it until 1891. Then the lease was undertaken by Robert Arthur, owner of the Royal Court Theatre, London, the Theatre Royal, Newcastle-on-Tyne, the Theatre Royal, Nottingham and Her Majesty's Theatre, Dundee. In 1897, he purchased the theatre outright and the Aberdeen Theatre and Opera Company went into liquidation, settling all its debts.

These early years saw a succession of high-quality musicals and drama performances. In 1886, for example, the first visit to the city by the D'Oyly Carte Opera Company brought Gilbert and Sullivan's operetta *The Mikado*. A footnote in the advance publicity ordered that 'bonnets should not be worn in the Orchestra Stalls and the first three rows of the Dress Circle'.

With new regulations regarding fire and the safety of patrons, Arthur undertook a complete reconstruction of Her Majesty's, this time commissioning the services of the finest architect of British theatres, Frank Matcham. His sumptuous decor, wonderful acoustics and sightlines are still in place today and the building, later

Images of Aberdeen's first Opera House as restored by Frank Matcham in 1897

Above and right: Matcham's sweeping balconies

The beautiful ceiling stained with nicotine

A vision created by Jim Brooks of how The Tivoli would look if it is ever restored to its former glory

Matcham's extravagance
above the boxes

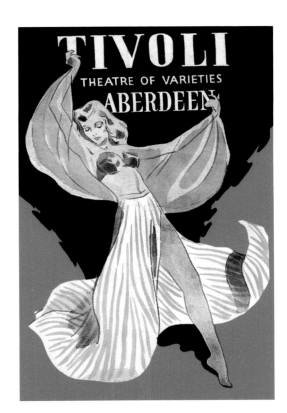

Tivoli flyer

Still set out for bingo

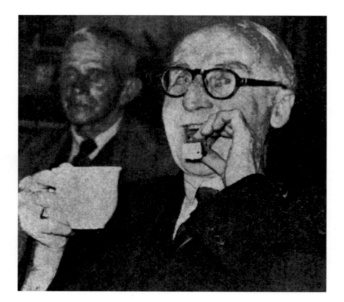

Haydn P. Halstead

Clifford Jordan –
popular musical
director

renamed the Tivoli Theatre, is regarded as one of the nation's greatest treasures.
The Theatres Trust acclaims it as 'a Sleeping Beauty awaiting awakening'. The
same organisation has recently revised its assessment of the building and now
believes that more of the original Phipps architecture is in place than first thought,
making it even more important as a national treasure.

As the popularity of theatre-going grew, Robert Arthur saw the need for a larger
venue with greater seating capacity, improved refreshment areas, better comfort for
the patrons and more appropriate staging facilities to accommodate the grander
touring productions. His eye fell on a piece of ground on Rosemount Viaduct next
to the Schoolhill Railway Station. The story of His Majesty's Theatre was about to
begin.

With his interest now concentrated on his new theatre, Robert Arthur set
about closing and disposing of Her Majesty's. The curtain came down on Saturday,
1 December 1906, after the final performance of the comedy *A Country Mouse* by
Arthur Law. Certain conditions were attached to the sale that prevented the theatre

from presenting plays and pantomimes and condemned it to life as a variety house. Imposed by Robert Arthur to prevent competition with his new His Majesty's, this harsh restrictive measure remained in force. It was even discussed in the House of Lords on Tuesday, 2 July 1940.

Will Fyffe

After considerable alterations and refurbishment and renamed the Tivoli Theatre of Variety, the building reopened on the Aberdeen July holiday in 1910. It had been taken over by a group of prominent Aberdeen businessmen led by James Leith. In charge of bookings was a Glasgow theatrical agent, Horace Collins. Walter Gilbert moved from the Palace Theatre in Bridge Place to become its first manager, with Jack Shepherd as musical director, a post he held until his death in 1921. During the First World War, the revue *Bobo* was very popular, returning for many seasons. The producer was William McFarland, of McFarland's Musical Hall fame, and the star of the show was a young and then unknown comedian, Will Fyffe.

Shepherd was succeeded in 1921 by Haydn P. Halstead, also from the Palace. A brilliant musician, he composed and orchestrated 'I Belong to Glasgow' which became Fyffe's theme tune. This quintessentially Glaswegian song was, in fact, composed by an Aberdonian with words written – and performed to great acclaim – by a man from Dundee!

After fourteen years, Halstead was followed by Clark Brown, then by a Mr Kendall and eventually by perhaps the theatre's best-known musical director, Clifford Jordan of the original Marcliffe Hotel.

The Tivoli enjoyed great success as a variety house, bringing a host of top stars

The eccentric Dr Walford Bodie played whatever theatre offered him the best box office returns, thus exerting his authority as one of the biggest crowd pullers of his day.

Bills advertising shows from lesser theatres

of the day to the city. In his recollections of the early period of the theatre, Angus McPhail recalls The Craggs, a clever tumbling act of a father and his four sons, the popular magicians David Devant, The Maskalynes, Horace Goldin and the outstanding Chung Ling Soo. Although he maintained a Chinese identity, Chung Ling Soo was, in fact, an Englishman of Scottish descent who had been born William E. Robinson. He specialised in a bullet-catching trick, catching marked bullets in a plate held in his hand. On 23 March 1918, a week after appearing at the Tivoli, he was repeating the trick at the Wood Green Empire, London, when he slipped up and was shot dead in full view of the audience.

A huge favourite was Dr Walford Bodie, from nearby Macduff, who thrilled audiences not only with sleight of hand, disappearing magic and electric stunts but also with eccentric showmanship and publicity gimmicks. Another popular star was the Australian singer Florrie Forde, who completed twelve sell-out seasons at the Tivoli. Her long career ended in Aberdeen in April 1940, when she died while travelling in a taxi after a performance given to wounded servicemen at Kingseat Hospital. It fell to her good friend Harry Milne, manager of the Tivoli at the time, to arrange her funeral.

Comedians galore helped to establish the Tivoli as a favourite in the hearts of Aberdeen audiences. Among them were Dave Willis, Alec Finlay, Jack Radcliffe, Vivian Foster 'The Vicar of Mirth' and Albert Whelan – who always made his entrances and exits whistling the tune 'Lustige Bruder' ('Jolly Brothers'), thus setting a trend for signature tunes. Comic stars in later years included Lex McLean, Tommy Morgan, Johnny Victory, Ron Dale, Andy Stewart and the Logan Family. There were also appearances at the theatre by George Formby, Fred Kitchen, Flotsam and Jetsam, Layton and Johnston, Clapham and Dwyer, Carl Brisson, Albert Sandler, De Groot and Donald Peers. Some claim that Charlie Chaplin performed there with Fred Carno's 'Mumming Birds' but there is no evidence to support this.

Highlights from the great days of the Tivoli

Calum Kennedy, the great entertainer who was
the last owner of the Tivoli Variety Theatre

Naughton and Gold

A souvenir of a charity performance to raise funds
for the victims of the Torry ferry disaster

Billy Cotton

Dave Willis

Jack Milroy and Mary Lee

In May 1938, the Tivoli was purchased by James A. Collins, the Glasgow theatrical agent, for the sum of £9,000. On his death, his shares were taken over by local architect T. Scott Sutherland and the theatre continued successfully until 1954 when it was sold once more, this time for £50,000, to a Glasgow syndicate headed by W. R. Galt. He introduced the resident variety show featuring the Logans, Jack Milroy and Alec Finlay. With them came future stars such as Kathy Kay, Dennis Willis, the Kay Sisters and Margo Henderson.

In the 1960s, the Tivoli hit some lean years, sometimes closing for as long as eight weeks. Local bookmaker George Duncan offered to take it on to run bingo sessions but this prompted protest from the actors' trade union, Equity. The popular Scottish entertainer Calum Kennedy stepped into the breach, forming Grampian Theatre Holdings in 1965 with directors Anne Lorne Gillies, Ross Bowie and various local businessmen. But the venture was short-lived and, on Saturday, 2 April 1966, the Tivoli finally closed its doors. First Leisure Bingo from Perth took over the building and kept it in good order until 1999 when the building was sold to local businessman Anthony Donald for £150,000.

In 2000, the Scottish Arts Council identified the need in Aberdeen for a medium-sized theatre, seating around 650 patrons. With this in mind, a group of amateur drama enthusiasts established the Tivoli Steering Group to investigate bringing the Tivoli Theatre back to life to fulfil this need. Hence, the Tivoli Trust was formed as a registered charity. At the time of writing, the trust is negotiating with the owner to purchase the building so that funding can be raised locally and nationally. The Trust proposes to bring mid-scale professional productions to the city, to provide a more viable home for large-scale amateur productions, to establish a centre for our own north-east culture and to investigate seriously the establishment of a repertory theatre. Success will mean that an important part of Aberdeen's cultural heritage would be saved and restored.

Dave Allen, Resident Stage Manager, who along with his brother Bert was associated with the Tivoli for many years. Dave is pictured in his office with his collection of signed photographs of the many stars who became his friends.

Johnny Beattie

Robert Wilson

Jimmy Shand – the King of Scottish music

The Lesser Theatres

Other theatres were erected around the city but most of these were music halls, low variety houses and circuses.

In 1888, a church, at the foot of Market Street, known locally as 'the Tarty Kirk', was converted into a popular vaudeville theatre. It was initially named McFarland's Music Hall and later became the Alhambra Theatre. It was converted to a zoo in 1907. It then turned into a cycle shop and later housed the premises of H. G. Drummond & Co., Belting Manufacturers.

A disreputable venue appeared in 1911 on Albion Street (now the Beach Boulevard), which was referred to locally as Bool Road since it led to a bowling green down at the Links. The 'Bool Theatre', better known as 'The Penny Rattler', was the scene of many a rowdy performance and often incurred the wrath of the local magistrates.

Scott's Theatre in John Street was best known for its association with the magician John Anderson, who went on to find great fame throughout the country billed as 'The Wizard of the North'. He was the son-in-law of the proprietor, a Mr Scott, who taught him the 'gun trick' that became the sensational finale to his act. In the trick, a marked ball was placed in a gun and fired. Anderson was the target! After the smoke from the firing had cleared, Anderson was seen holding the same marked ball in his hand. He was a conjuror of high standing and Harry Houdini, the world-famous escapologist, admired him so much that, in 1914, he made a pilgrimage to Anderson's grave in St Nicholas Graveyard in Aberdeen. Houdini was photographed standing beside the grave and he was so appalled by its derelict state that he arranged for the Magicians' Club in London to raise funds for its maintenance.

Cooke's Royal Circus, at the corner of Summer Street and Union Street, began

The site of the Alhambra Theatre just off Market Street

The site of Cooke's Royal Circus
on the corner of Summer Street

The Penny Rattler in Albion Street

Above: This is believed to be the interior of the Palace Theatre

Right: The Palace Theatre on Bridge Place

in 1842, becoming Gilcomston South Church after the circus moved to Bridge Place in 1888. In 1893, it became the People's Palace and, on 30 September 1896, there was a disastrous fire in which seven young boys perished. Like a phoenix, it arose from the flames in 1898 as the New Palace Theatre and continued to have a very successful life. The earliest *Student Shows*, so popular with Aberdeen audiences, were staged there. One of them starred the well-loved actor Andrew Cruickshank, who later became famous as Dr Cameron in the television series *Dr Finlay's Casebook*. By 1929, the New Palace's glory had faded and it was sold to the Edinburgh promoter Jack Poole, who ran it successfully as a popular cinema. Today, like so many other grand buildings in the city, it has a new lease of life as a nightclub.

The New Beach Pavilion being built in 1928

Pierrots, in the open in all
kinds of weather

Inside the original Beach Pavilion built in 1905

HARRY GORDON

ALICE STEPHENSON

JACK HOLDEN

Harry Gordon, Alice Stephenson and Jack Holden

Harry in character

Harry Gordon and the Beach Pavilion

In the early days, entertainment at Aberdeen's beach was a hazardous affair, at the mercy of inclement weather. (Yes, it did sometimes rain in those days.) On rainy days, the Pierrot shows that were performed in the open or on the bandstand at the Queen's Links would lose their audiences and, as a result, their income. This problem was addressed by David Thomson, an Aberdeen coachman with a flair for entertainment. In May 1905, he opened Aberdeen's first Beach Pavilion, a wooden and corrugated-iron hall on the Esplanade. Thomson had a great belief in the young talent of the city and encouraged youngsters to present turns in the new venue. However, he incurred the wrath of some citizens who felt it was improper for children to be performing their 'party pieces' in public.

Harry Gordon

His investment proved to be a sound one. Apart from establishing a tradition of clean family entertainment with top stars from all over the country, one of his popular talent shows in 1911 starred a young boy from the city who was to become a household name – Harry Gordon. After the death of Thomson in 1921 and the retirement of his widow in 1923, Harry took over the lease of the building, along with Thomson's sister Cissie Murray. Together, they ran a most successful programme until 1927, when the Esplanade was rebuilt and the old pavilion was pulled down. It was replaced by the more substantial New Beach Pavilion, on the other side of the road, nearer to Footdee. Built by Aberdeen Town Council at a cost of £9,000, the new pavilion had a capacity of 750 and was leased to Harry Gordon and Cissie Murray, opening on Friday, 4 May 1928.

It was here that the Harry Gordon Entertainers set the standard for seaside

Harry pioneered troupes of dancing girls in seaside revue

Some of Harry's own cartoons

Harry, portrayed on his publicity material by another cartoonist

entertainment – not only for Aberdeen but also for the whole of Scotland. Harry introduced the 'quickie sketch' and his glamorous chorus girls, combined with good clean entertainment, proved very popular with holiday families. He also built up a regular clientele, whom he described in a song:

> Fittie folk, Kitty folk,
> Country folk and city folk,
> Folk fae Constitution Street and
> Folk fae Rubislaw Den,
> Wallfield, Nellfield,
> Mannofield and Cattofield . . .

Harry Gordon exercised strict control over the content of his shows. Every performer had his or her material vetted for any content that might be offensive or considered in dubious taste. The blue pencil was used vigorously to ensure that the time-honoured tradition of clean family entertainment continued. It was even applied to some of the biggest names from British variety when they performed at the Pavilion. Flotsam and Jetsam, Flanagan and Allen, Gertrude Lawrence and Jack Warner all had to toe Harry's line. Apart from these notable guest artistes, the backbone of the Pavilion's success was the resident company, which included Harry, his feeds Jack Holden and Clem Ashby and the ever-faithful Alice Stephenson at the piano. Harry's catchphrase, ''S cold today', may have referred to the weather outside but never to the warm and happy atmosphere inside.

The advent of the Second World War brought an end to Harry's reign at the Pavilion. Bombs were dropped on the beach in the early days of 1940, dissuading audiences from making the journey. Around the same time, the Town Council decided that huge profits were being made by the lessees and raised the rent

Left: Harry as a Dame

Right: Harry as The Provost

beyond what Harry and Cissie were willing to pay. Harry moved on to bigger Scottish stages and established himself as a national star.

The Pavilion closed for the duration of the war, reopening in 1946 with Murray Stewart as manager and Archie McCulloch as lessee. This pair ran it until 1951, when it was leased by the Donald Family. Big names continued to tread the boards there, including Dave Willis, the Beverly Sisters, Kay Cavendish, Julie Andrews, Morecambe and Wise, Anne Ziegler and Webster Booth, Bob and Alf Pearson, Dick Emery and Harry Locke, but the writing was on the wall and the appeal was fading. In 1955, local businessman Ernest Buchan took up the challenge and kept the Pavilion alive until 1961, when it was sold and reopened as the Gaiety restaurant. The building still stands today as a Jimmy Chung's restaurant and continues to contribute to the revitalisation of the Beach Esplanade.

Two new theatres in Aberdeen, although outwith the original remit of this book, deserve a mention. The Arts Centre in King Street, which opened in 1963 in the former North Church, is a very popular venue for local amateur groups and small-scale professional touring companies. And the Lemon Tree, next door in West North Street, is well known nationally as a music venue but also presents touring productions in its small studio theatre.

Frank Matcham

Theatre Architect

1854–1920

After an apprenticeship in Torquay, Matcham joined the London firm of Jethro T. Robinson, who was the consultant theatre architect to the Lord Chamberlain. He married Robinson's daughter and took over the firm in 1878, the year in which new regulations were enacted regarding fire and the safety of patrons.

Thereafter, Matcham's success was unbounded and he went on to become the most prolific theatre architect of all time. Despite his enormous output, he developed a very personal style that is instantly recognisable. He was a supreme example of the unacademic architect who became a master of his craft. He could always be relied on to deliver a lively, sensuous interior, inexpensively constructed, while remaining acutely aware of the technical difficulties of sightlines, acoustics and structure. As well as patenting lifts and concentric cantilevers for theatre balconies, he had a remarkable grasp of the three-dimensional possibilities of auditorium design, using every trick to maximum effect – dipping balconies, stage boxes stepping down and set forwards and backwards to improve the sight line – and the whole composition would be awash with a cornucopia of drapery and decoration.

Regarded today as a near-genius, he created the original designs for some eighty theatres, of which almost half have been lost, and he remodelled a further eighty, of which twenty-eight survive. Outstanding examples of his work, apart from his two theatres in Aberdeen, include the Hackney Empire in London and the King's Theatre, Glasgow.

One of Matcham's grandest gestures was to design a new wing for Brinsworth House, a retirement home run by the Variety Artistes' Benevolent Fund, for which he charged no fee.

Frank Matcham

The original Matcham design showing twin towers and
an ornamental gateway giving access to the rear of the theatre

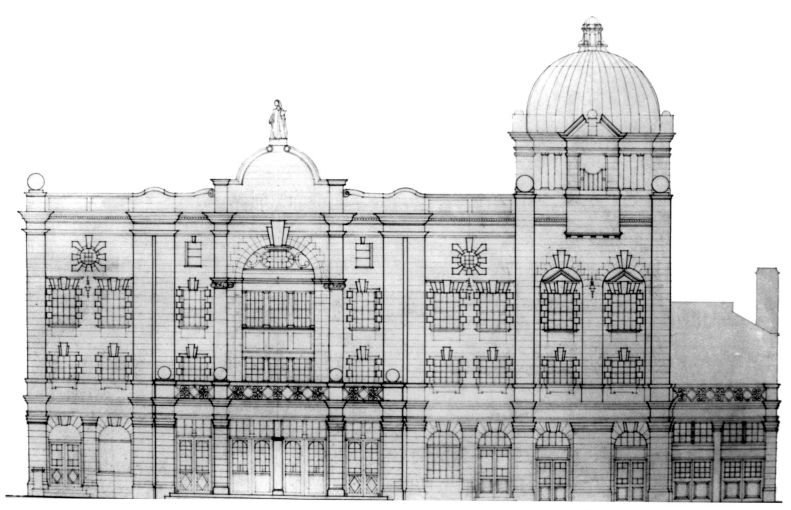

The new design for the facade

Act One

The Birth of His Majesty's Theatre

At first sight, the prestigious site at the head of Union Terrace Gardens might have appeared to be inappropriate for the erection of a theatre. Facing on to a viaduct, there was a considerable drop to the Denburn Valley and Black's Buildings below. An added difficulty was the Denburn, which ran through one corner of the site. The architect Frank Matcham, commissioned by Robert Arthur, seized the opportunity to produce a feature which was unique in British theatre design – a foyer entrance that leads directly to the Dress Circle, which holds the best seats in the house. He also used the slope of the site to marry with the rake of the auditorium and create vast storage areas under the stage.

However, the birth of His Majesty's was fraught with setbacks. Matcham's first design – a largely symmetrical building with small towers at each end of the facade – was not greeted with great enthusiasm by the planners in 1901. Because of a shortage of Kemnay granite, building did not commence until 1904, after a completely new design had been submitted. The architectural style of this new design is difficult to pinpoint. Certainly Matcham's ambition was for a grand statement. He blended early Georgian – very fashionable at that time – with touches of decorative baroque to produce a building which, rather than heralding a breakthrough in architectural design, certainly held its own with its impressive neighbours to the west.

In the workshop of James Scott & Sons, craftsmen are finishing the statues designed by William Buchan

The view from the lower level of Union Terrace Gardens is certainly quite stunning. The Kemnay granite of the facade sparkles in the sun with the soft green verdigris of the copper dome, said to be placed there to balance the dome of the church next door, creating a beautiful silhouette against the sky. The curved gable above the central parapet at the front entrance is topped with an imposing statue of Tragedy and Comedy, by a Mr Arrowsmith, a London sculptor, although the sword depicting Tragedy has long since disappeared. In the 1980s, this statue, which is constructed of reinforced concrete, was found to have split down its length. It now wears a corset of brass bands! Perhaps in the future some benefactor will provide the funds to replace the sword.

The opening date was set for Monday, 3 December 1906, but this came under threat when the magistrates expressed concern, during their site-inspection the week prior to opening, over certain safety measures that had not been completed. A further inspection two days later revealed that the workmen had pulled out all the stops and a licence was granted. Pride had won through for this was largely an Aberdeen theatre built by Aberdeen tradesmen.

Here Scott's men are working on the ceiling of the foyer

Garnet Fraser's photograph
of the partly built theatre

The list is impressive:

Masonry:	A. Anderson
Slating:	G. Farquhar
Joinery:	Henry & Keith
Electrics:	Aberdeen Electric Company
Plastering:	James Scott & Son
Upholstery:	Councillor R. W. Wishart
Sculpture:	W. Buchan
Marble:	Whitehead & Son
Painting:	Donald & Son
Plumbing:	Walter Simpson
Draperies & Furnishings:	Cranston & Elliot, Edinburgh

The Opening Night

Monday, 3 December 1906

Mr Robert
Arthur

The opening night created great excitement in the city. All the reserved seats were sold out well in advance and the crowd queuing for the unreserved seats was so great that Chief Constable Anderson was summoned with a large force of constables to ensure that everything was under control.

Inside, Matcham's expertise was revealed in its full glory. Fine-grained Italian marble, polished mahogany timbers and elegant plaster decorations – quite restrained and refined compared to most of Matcham's earlier work in other theatres – combined with sumptuous red velvet drapes and seating, offset by an off-white colour scheme. All was greatly admired by that first-night audience.

Three graceful curved balconies, the Dress Circle, Upper Circle and Balcony, and a raked stalls area – linked to a one-in-thirty-four shallow stage rake – provided the near-perfect sightlines for which Matcham was famous. The acoustics were greatly enhanced by highly reflective tiling in a richly coloured tulip design around the Stalls area – an important feature in the days before electronic sound amplification. Further statues of Tragedy and Comedy, elegantly sculpted by William Buchan of Belmont Street, Aberdeen, stood above the two tiers of boxes on either side of the marble proscenium arch. These sit well

The opening night programme

The Auditorium

The Foyer

with Buchan's finely modelled frieze, 'The Goddess of Drama' high above the proscenium arch.

Unique among British theatres is the circular Dress Circle Bar with its marble counter – a real piece of Matcham magic. Other bars in the Stalls, the Upper Circle and Balcony amply catered for the needs of theatregoers. Separation of the 'rough' and the 'smooth' was important in the early twentieth century. The Stalls Bar was mainly a beer bar (complete with spitoons!) catering for the Pit Stalls. Horseshoe-shaped, with an elegant wooden screen across its base, it had hatches where more refined beverages were served to the more elegant customers sitting in the Orchestra Stalls. In the auditorium, a wooden fence confined the riff-raff to their own area. Separate entrances for the 'early doors' ensured they did not clash with the rich and powerful arriving in their carriages at the main doors.

At that time, the backstage accommodation was of the highest standard. A wide stage, running from the proscenium to the back wall, was graced by an onstage paint frame with a glazed sloping roof. The flying grid, with forty-two sets of lines of hemp rope, towered some sixty feet above the stage. A tall scenery dock door at stage level alongside the property store allowed easy access for awkward scenery

The Dress Circle Bar

The Stalls Bar

arriving from the Schoolhill railway station next door. Twelve dressing rooms at the Prompt Side of the stage ranged from 'star' rooms at stage level to large 'chorus' rooms upstairs. Under the stage and auditorium was a vast cellar, providing one of the largest scenery stores in a provincial theatre. With its side and back walls built from Tillyfourie granite and its special lightweight concrete floors, His Majesty's Theatre met the highest standards of fire safety.

When opening night finally arrived, every seat was filled, with the patrons in the Dress Circle and Orchestra Stalls resplendent in full evening dress. An air of anticipation awaited the entrance of the musical director. Promptly at 7.30 p.m. he entered, the orchestra struck up and the rich red velvet and gold house curtain rose to the opening number of the pantomime, *Little Red Riding Hood*. This production really cannot be compared to a modern panto with its obligatory appearance by a television or sports personality. Originally called *Sweet Red Riding Hood*, as revealed by a copy of Frank Dix's script, it was more of a musical play, which the local press

The Balcony Bar   The Upper Circle Bar

declared 'pretty and refined'. It had plenty of 'clean harmless mirth' for the children and 'an even higher appeal in the artistic beauty of the production' for the adults. It ran for four hours on its opening night, necessitating severe cuts for its run throughout the festive season.

Despite its length, the audience was so impressed they gave it three curtain calls, after which Robert Arthur appeared on stage to thunderous applause. In his speech, he asked the audience, 'Does it please you?' This was greeted with even more applause and he went on to explain, 'This is an Aberdeen playhouse built by Aberdeen workmen and is a credit to their handiwork.' Every member of the audience had been presented with a little booklet, *The Playhouse of Bon Accord*, written by Arthur, which traced the history of theatre in the City of Aberdeen up to the building of His Majesty's. In closing, he wrote these prophetic words, 'Now it remains with the people of Aberdeen to put the copestone of success on what the craftsmen of Aberdeen have builded with such care.'

Harry Adair Nelson

The first manager of the theatre was Harry Adair Nelson who had been headhunted by Robert Arthur. With a background of theatre ownership at the Prince of Wales in Liverpool, Nelson had had a highly respected career as the number one touring manager with the famous George Edwardes' Company. In her book *North East Folk*, his daughter Elizabeth Adair describes him as a well-dressed figure – his suits were made by W. J. Milne and his lace-up boots of the softest leather were specially made for him by Dunns. With starched wing-collars, a bow-tie and always wearing a carnation in his buttonhole, he would pop on his bowler hat, pick up his cane (often a sword-stick in case of footpads!) and set out at 6 p.m. prompt from his home at 65 Osborne Place for his walk to catch the tram at the corner of Prince Arthur Street, alighting at Union Terrace.

Although he was among the kindest of men and immensely popular, his daughter reports that he was a strict disciplinarian. One can imagine his anger when, during a performance of the popular *Student Show*, a riotous section of the audience armed with hockey sticks heckled the cast mercilessly, invaded the bar and smashed all the glasses. The orgy of destruction was only ended by the arrival of the police. The next day, he imposed a ban on students. Representations were made to plead for forgiveness but H. Adair Nelson was adamant and it was many years before the embargo was lifted.

During those early years, His Majesty's was run not only with clockwork precision but also with an air of sophisticated elegance. When carriages arrived at the front door, the doorman would step forward (with an umbrella in inclement weather), open the carriage door and escort the patrons into the foyer. Hats and coats would be deposited with the attendants and the patrons escorted to their seats in the Dress Circle, Parterre and Orchestra Stalls. The carriages would then depart

Harry Adair Nelson

to line the roads up Rosemount, down
Mount Street and along Westburn
Road as far as the Victoria Park.

At the end of the show, pageboys
would be dispatched, running along
the lines of carriages until they found
the number of the carriage matching the number on their ticket. They would then
hang on to the tailboard for the trip back to the theatre, pick up another ticket and
run back along the line – woe betide them if Nelson caught them riding the
carriages. Obviously it was dangerous for the young lads and he did not approve of
such risks being taken. Patrons seated in other parts of the theatre were treated
with equal courtesy though they were segregated – there were separate entrances
for the Upper Circle, Pit Stalls and Balcony.

Shows from the Early Years

The programme at this time was a varied and popular one. There were performances by many of the notable touring companies of the day and by international companies such as the Italian Royal Opera Company in July 1912 and the Imperial Russian Ballet Company in October 1913. Admission prices varied widely:

Orchestra Stalls – 4/-

Dress Circle – 3/-

Parterre Stalls – 3/-

Upper Circle – 2/-

Pit – 1/-

Balcony – 6d

Programmes cost one shilling and, if you came after 9 p.m., admission was half-price.

Whilst the visiting companies were made welcome, there were strict rules about how they behaved in the theatre. Artistes could only enter and leave by the Stage Door and visitors were strictly controlled.

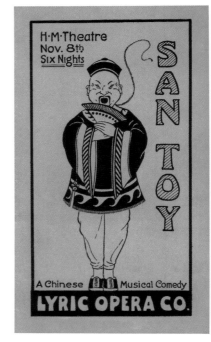

An early show

Some companies did excellent business whilst others barely covered their expenses and this is reflected in the contract made between the resident and touring company managers. The O'Mara Opera Company grossed over £800 for the week of 24 March 1917 (good business when the above ticket prices are taken into consideration) and

This notice from the Dress Circle Bar gives a flavour of the attitude at the time

Frank Dix, author

Jullien H. Wilson,
composer

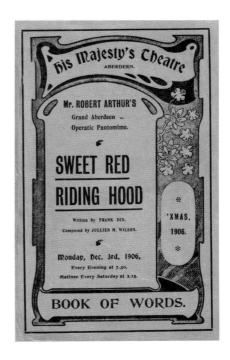
Sweet Red Riding Hood

subsequently left with sixty-five per cent of the box-office takings. Two weeks earlier, the play *Little Minister* had only grossed £270 and the company received only fifty-five per cent.

Touring companies made a great effort to ensure value for money during their visits. The O'Mara Opera Company performed thirteen different operas during a two-week visit in 1924 while, in 1926, the Henry Baynton Company performed eight Shakespeare plays in a single week. Close investigation also reveals that the same pieces of scenery appeared in many different shows – the spoken or sung word was obviously much more important than scenic spectacle! The cash books in which returns were recorded reveal that, for almost all shows, performances on Wednesday and Saturday evenings were by far the best attended.

Some early shows

A WARNING TO WOMEN
BY G. WATSON MILL.

HIS MAJESTY'S THEATRE
ABERDEEN
Monday, September 20th, 1909, for Six Nights
Matinee Saturday

ACT III. "You shall have the three thousand."

Mr. GEORGE ALEXANDER'S COMPANY
IN
"The Builder of Bridges"
A New Play in Four Acts by ALFRED SUTRO
FROM THE ST. JAMES'S THEATRE, LONDON

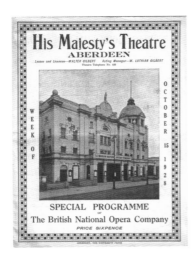

His Majesty's Theatre
ABERDEEN
Lessee and Licensee—WALTER GILBERT   Acting Manager—W. LOTHIAN GILBERT
Theatre Telephone No. 628

WEEK OF OCTOBER 15 1928

SPECIAL PROGRAMME
OF
The British National Opera Company
PRICE SIXPENCE

ABERDEEN: THE UNIVERSITY PRESS.

His Majesty's Theatre
ABERDEEN
Lessee and Licensee—WALTER GILBERT   Acting Manager—W. LOTHIAN GILBERT
Theatre Telephone No. 628

WEEK OF DECEMBER 8 1930

SPECIAL SOUVENIR PROGRAMME
OF THE
D'OYLY CARTE OPERA COMPANY
PRICE SIXPENCE

ABERDEEN: THE UNIVERSITY PRESS.

*The Performances during the
Aberdeen Little Theatre Guild Week
are as follows :—*

Monday, Thursday, and Saturday Evenings—
"LEAN HARVEST"
By RONALD JEANS

Tuesday and Wednesday Evenings—
"THE IMMORTAL LADY"
By CLIFFORD BAX

Friday Evening and Saturday Matinee—
"TWELFTH NIGHT"
By WILLIAM SHAKESPEARE

EVENING PERFORMANCES COMMENCE AT 7.45
MATINEE AT 2.30

BOOK NOW

Walter S. Gilbert

Walter S. Gilbert

In 1912, Robert Arthur leased the programming to Walter Gilbert from the Tivoli and, throughout the First World War, he brought many revues to His Majesty's. These featured the hit tunes of the day, including 'Alexander's Ragtime Band', 'Everbody's Doing It' and 'Alice Blue Gown'.

By 1923, Robert Arthur had become closely associated with the production company and theatrical agency Howard & Wyndham. He decided to sell the theatre to Mr Gilbert who wished to install his son Lothian as manager. H. Adair Nelson then departed for the Palace Theatre in Bridge Place, moving again a few years later to take over the management of the Royal Lyceum Theatre in Edinburgh. However, he was taken ill and returned home to Aberdeen, where he died in April 1929.

The Gilberts introduced many high-calibre variety shows to His Majesty's with stars including Harry Lauder, Neil Kenyon – a rising star promoted by Lauder – Tommy Handley, Harry Tate, Gracie Fields and Aberdeen's own 'Laird of Inversnecky' Harry Gordon, who filled the theatre to the roof. On one notable occasion, the French boxing champion Georges Carpentier gave an exhibition – it is said that ladies fainted as he feinted on stage!

Walter Gilbert died in 1931 and His Majesty's Theatre was put up for sale. Some feared that the building would be converted for some other use and there was an outcry from local theatregoers and from the stage fraternity. The variety star Sir Harry Lauder bemoaned its possible loss. The actor Matheson Lang declared it 'one of the finest theatres in the land'. C. B. Cochrane pledged that, if Aberdonians responded to save their theatre, he would bring his London production of Noel Coward's musical comedy *Bitter Sweet* at his own expense. A share issue was announced, with 30,000 shares at one pound each, and the Aberdeen Theatre

Neon lighting and a revolving stage
were installed by J. F. Donald in 1933

Company Ltd was formed. This venture later faltered and all monies were
refunded.

Thus His Majesty's remained in limbo until 1933 when Mr James Donald, a
local businessman, bought the theatre and founded a dynasty which would ever
afterwards be associated with the best of entertainment in Aberdeen.

The Donald Family

The Founder of the Dynasty
James Forrest Donald

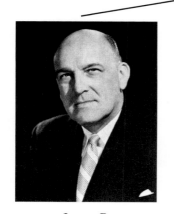

James R.

Herbert M.

Peter J.

Richard M.

James F.

Peter B.

The Donald Dynasty

THE SIGN OF (JFD) GOOD ENTERTAINMENT

James Forrest Donald was an excellent example of a self-made man. Born in Newhills, he came to the city to serve his apprenticeship as a coachbuilder with John Clark in Rose Street, later moving to the Great North of Scotland Railway Company at Kittybrewster. He was an enthusiastic dancer, founding the Gondolier Dancing Club in the small Albert Hall in Huntly Street. So successful was he as an instructor of step and ballroom dancing that he decided to make it his career, establishing the Gondolier Hall in North Silver Street, which became the best-known dancing school in the north of Scotland.

Despite his breezy, genial nature, J. F. Donald was a strict disciplinarian on the dance floor and successive generations of young Aberdonians were taught not only dancing but also deportment and correct behaviour in the ballroom. For thirty years he was a leading member of the British Association of Dancing and he became its president in 1921. He was also an outstanding athlete on the cycling track, winning many races as a member of the Aberdeen Abstainers' Cycling Club.

His greatest success, however, was in developing cinema entertainment in the city. His first cinema was the West End, which later became the Playhouse, on Union Street. He later built the Grand Central in George Street, purchased the Picturedrome, opposite the Central Library, renaming it the Cinema House, and he then bought the Queen's Cinema on the corner of Back Wynd and Union Street.

At this time, he was also a highly respected member of the town council, representing St Nicholas Ward in 1927. In 1928, after redistribution of the wards, he was elected to represent Gilcolmston. His charity work was outstanding – he organised many charity concerts to raise funds for the poor, in particular helping to fund the work of Oakbank School for Boys, of which he was a director.

The proudest moment of his life was when he stood on the stage of His Majesty's Theatre on 14 August 1933 to invite Lord Provost Alexander to declare the theatre open after its purchase and refurbishment. At a cost of £35,000 for the purchase and £10,000 for refurbishment, he had converted the building to operate as both a cinema and a theatre. He had installed a cinema projector and a revolving stage – the only one in Scotland – and had changed the rake of the seats in the Upper Circle and Balcony to improve the sightlines for watching films. He had also installed new seats, carpets and furnishings, used spray-painting for the first time in Aberdeen and outlined the facade with the largest neon sign in Scotland. Such was the respect he enjoyed that he was able, with the support of tradesmen throughout the city, to complete the whole project in sixteen weeks!

Those tradesmen were:

S. B. Russell, Affleck Street:	Building Work
J. & A. Ogilvie, 369 Union Street:	Curtains and Drapes
D. MacAndrew & Co., 120 Loch Street:	Joinery
R. S. Donald, 15 Rosemount Viaduct:	Carpeting
E. Copland, 4b Crown Terrace:	Spray-Painting
Farquhar & Gill, Loch Street:	Paint Materials
Alexander McKay, 41 The Green:	Electrical Works
Forbes Gordon, 23 Diamond Street:	Plumbing

James Forrest Donald did not live long enough to see his enterprise grow. After several months of illness, he died on 4 March 1934 at his home in North Silver Street, aged sixty-four. He was held in such esteem by the public that thousands lined the streets to pay their respects to his funeral cortege on its way to St Peter's Cemetery. He was survived by his widow Elizabeth, his partner in all his ventures, until 1946. Thereafter, the company, James F. Donald (Aberdeen Cinemas), continued under the directorship of his four sons, James Riddel Donald, Herbert Milne Donald, Peter John Donald and Richard Milne Donald. They went on to develop the company into the leading entertainment group in north-east Scotland. Apart from His Majesty's, they controlled the Playhouse, the Capitol, the Majestic, the Cinema House, the Queen's, the Belmont, the Casino, the Torry Cinema, the Astoria, the City Cinema, the Grand Central, the Kingsway, the Beach Pavilion, the Ice Rink, the Picture House in Stonehaven and the Victoria Cinema in Inverurie.

Peter J. Donald took over at His Majesty's Theatre, while James R. Donald continued to direct and tutor at the Gondolier Academy. With the outbreak of war in 1939, Peter volunteered and was commissioned in the Gordon Highlanders, serving with them until the end of hostilities in 1945. During this time, James ran the theatre and did so very successfully, attracting many outstanding artistes during those difficult years. Peter took over again briefly after the war but moved south to join Howard & Wyndham, becoming general manager and chairman in 1966 and managing director in 1972. He retired in 1975 but continued as a consultant.

James thus became manager of His Majesty's in 1948 and set the standards for care and attention to hospitality which visiting artistes came to associate with the theatre.

That personal touch became legend in the British theatre industry. Dame Sybil Thorndike once remarked:

> It is the only theatre in which I have acted where, during a matinee, there
> will be a knock on my dressing-room door and there will be a tall man
> carrying a tray set with afternoon tea. It's never a manager, my dear.
> It's always one of the owners!

For her part, the French film star Leslie Caron managed to include the word 'divine' four times in a sentence describing Aberdeen and His Majesty's.

Courtesy and charm were accompanied by astute business acumen. Hearsay has it that, in days of gas emergency lighting, an attendant would be given one match to light all the lamps down one side of the auditorium! Andy Stewart once quipped that James Donald Jr treated Aberdeen's money as if it was his own. However, that canny business expertise kept the theatre's head above water through many difficult financial times. Alone among Scottish theatres, it survived until the 1970s as a privately owned concern, with no state assistance.

For many years, the Donald Family enjoyed a close relationship with Howard & Wyndam. As a result, many first-class touring companies visited Aberdeen either prior to or immediately following appearances in the West End of London. Aberdeen audiences were regarded as discerning judges of quality and many companies chose the Granite City because they knew they would be treated handsomely by the theatre management, the theatrical landladies and the 'punters' in the streets.

Great Shows and Great Stars

The shows that came to His Majesty's were of a quality that cannot be overstated.

Spend a few hours in the Central Library scanning through the collection of theatre programmes and the famous, familiar names leap from the pages. In December 1933, there was a production of *Mother of Pearl* starring Rex Harrison and Richard Murdoch. In September 1938, the impresario Prince Littler, master of many spectacular productions, presented *St Moritz*, Aberdeen's first ice show. The Whatmore Players made their debut in May 1939 with a repertory season originally intended to last six weeks – this was soon extended to seventeen. Noel Coward's comedy *Hay Fever* not only starred Stewart Granger and his wife Elspeth March but also brought the honeymooning couple Michael Dennison and Dulcie Gray to the city. Such was their affection for His Majesty's – and particularly for the smell of the polish used on the linoleum – that they returned on several occasions, culminating with Oscar Wilde's *The Importance of Being Earnest*, which also starred Penelope Keith.

They return with Penelope Keith in *The Importance of Being Earnest*

MICHAEL DENISON
Began acting with the O.U.D.S. playing in John Gielgud's production of "Richard II.," Orlando to Nova Pilbeam's Rosalind. Also played "Parnell" at the Webber-Douglas Dramatic School in London with Dulcie Gray as Kitty O'Shea. Went from school direct into the permanent Company of the London Mask Theatre where he has been playing a variety of parts under Michael Macowan since last September, one of which was Gordon in Priestley's "Dangerous Corner."

DULCIE GRAY
On completion of her training was quick to secure an engagement for leading parts with the Hunstanton Repertory and comes to Aberdeen after broadcasting with Nicholas Hannen on the National and Empire Programmes. Played Kitty O'Shea in "Parnell" at Webber-Douglas Dramatic School in London.

MARGOT LISTER
Trained at Lady Benson's School. Spent four years in Repertory Theatres. Toured with Matheson Lang in "The Chinese Bungalow." Played in Egypt in Robert Atkins' Shakespeare Season. Played in Shaw Plays with the Macdona Players. Played in Brandon-Thomas Seasons spending five years in Edinburgh and Glasgow.

DESMOND KEITH, R.A.D.A., 1928-9
"Elizabeth of England," Cambridge Theatre. With Yvonne Arnaud "Doctor's Orders," Globe Theatre. "Will You Love Me Always," Globe Theatre. "The Man Who Was Fed-Up," Vaudeville Theatre. "Silver Box," "Getting Married," Little! Theatre. "My Wife's Family," Garrick Theatre. "Ghost Train" Revival, Criterion Theatre. "Lord Adrian," Nichero. Gate Theatre. Hull Repertory Theatre. Henry Baynton Shakespearean Company. Eleven Television productions.

Michael and Dulcie in *Hay Fever* – on their honeymoon

Another popular repertory troupe was the Wilson Barrett Company. They were bombed out of their home in London in 1940 and moved to Edinburgh, playing at the city's Royal Lyceum Theatre and the Alhambra in Glasgow. They made their debut at His Majesty's in December 1947 with *Dear Octopus*, starring Richard Matthews and Phyllis Barker. A season ticket for the Wilson Barrett Company became a popular Christmas or birthday present for avid Aberdonian theatregoers. The company finally bowed out in August 1955.

The Whatmore Players returned in 1956 to play a long summer season under the direction of Dennis Ramsden, with his beautiful wife Christine Russell as star. Notable performers appearing during this period include Graham Ashley, Mollie Sugden, John Cater and Brian Cant. There were also beautiful sets by Ani Jasper and Sheila Ward.

Under the Donalds, the programme at His Majesty's more than catered for the broad tastes of an Aberdeen audience. From 1933 onwards, top stars and leading companies from across the spectrum graced its stage. Stars of variety, comedy and music included Tommy Trinder, Harry Lauder, Tommy Handley, Wee Georgie Wood, Layton and Johnston, the Good Companions, the Henry Hall Orchestra, Harry Gordon, Dave Willis, Jack Radcliffe, Jimmy Logan, Rikki Fulton, Jack Milroy, Stanley Baxter, Andy Stewart, the Fol-de-Rols, Max Bygraves, Rowan Atkinson, The Corries, Sade, Lulu, Spandau Ballet and Billy Connolly.

Opera was presented by the D'Oyly Carte Opera Company, the Italian Opera, the Carl Rosa Opera Company, the Sadler's Wells Opera Company and – after it was founded in 1962 – Scottish Opera. On 9 October 1972, Her Majesty, Queen Elizabeth, the Queen Mother came to the theatre for a performance by Scottish Opera of Donizetti's *Don Pasquale*.

There were also visits by internationally famous ballet companies, including Ballet Rambert, the Festival Ballet, the London Festival Ballet, London

Contemporary Dance Theatre, the Royal Ballet, Sierra Leone National Dance Company and the Spanish Dance Company. Formed in 1969, Scottish Ballet began visiting His Majesty's in 1974. Under the inspired direction of Peter Darrell, the company thrilled Aberdeen audiences with guest appearances by Dame Margot Fonteyn and Rudolph Nureyev and it gained royal patronage from Her Royal Highness, Princess Margaret.

Drama performances brought many star names, including Noel Coward in a season of his own plays, Roger Livesey in *Watch Over The Rhine*, Michael Redgrave in *Uncle Harry*, Robert Morley and Beatrice Lillie in *The Staff Dance*, Alastair Sim in *Mr Belfrey*, Cedric Hardwicke in *House on the Bridge*, Bebe Daniels in *Panama Hattie*, Sybil Thorndike and Emlyn Williams in *The Corn is Green* and many other great names from the West End stages including Robertson Hare, Fay Compton, Edith Evans, Ivor Novello, Alec Guinness, Diana Churchill, Eric Porter, Flora Robson, Anna Neagle, Evelyn Laye, Robert Beattie, Andrew Cruickshank. Hollywood stars came too: Vivien Leigh in Bernard Shaw's *The Doctor's Dilemma*; Tyrone Power in *The Devil's Disciple* by the same writer; and Charlton Heston in Robert Bolt's *A Man for All Seasons*.

Comedies were particularly popular and starred wonderful performers like Wilfred Hyde White, Jack Hulbert and Cicely Courtnedge, Jimmy Edwards and Eric Sykes, Duncan Macrae, Sylvia Sims, Richard Murdoch, Brian Murphy and Avril Angers.

As the popularity of spectacular musicals grew, many that were suited to the dimensions of a provincial theatre came to His Majesty's. These included *Jesus Christ Superstar*, *Godspell*, *Hair*, *Fiddler on the Roof*, *Elvis* and *Buddy Holly* from the modern era, as well as favourites from earlier years, among them *Desert Song* with John Hanson, *White Horse Inn*, *The Merry Widow*, *The Pyjama Game* and *Old Chelsea*.

Scottish entertainment was very popular at His Majesty's. This ranged from the

Andy Stewart – holder of
the record attendance

lavish and spectacular *Five Past Eight* productions, featuring two or three stars with
a large dance chorus and showgirls, to the more compact single-personality shows,
often backed by an onstage showband, produced and dressed in-house.

Andy Stewart packed them in during the summer of the typhoid epidemic in
1964 and set a record of 150,000 patrons for a summer season. Johnny Beattie, the
Alexander Brothers, Peter Morrison, Jim MacLeod, Jack Sinclair, Robbie
Shepherd, Kenneth McKellar and the *Fiddlers' Spectacular* all enjoyed enthusiastic
support. One of the greatest coups the Donalds pulled off was persuading the
members of a local revue group to try out at His Majesty's. Thus was born the
magic that was Scotland The What? – of which there will be more in a later
chapter.

Support for local talent was an essential part of programming from the early
days. Amateur groups appearing at His Majesty's included the Aberdeen Little
Theatre Guild, the Lyric Musical Society, Aberdeen Opera Company, the *Student
Show*, Jeannie Hendry, Miss Donaldson, Eileen Ewen, the Scouts' *Gang Show* and
in more recent years, the Limelight and Phoenix Theatre Companies.

Alec Finlay/
Rikki Fulton flyer

Jimmy Logan

The Corries

Sydney Devine

Jock Morgan – the finest comedian
to come from Kemnay

Bill McCue

Kenneth McKellar

Peter Morrison

Jim Macleod

Stanley Baxter

Fiona Kennedy

Royal visits to the theatre are occasions for
great rejoicing and civic and public pride

King Edward VII and Queen Alexandra, having opened Marischal College, drove past but did not come in

Right: The Queen Mother is welcomed to His Majesty's by two pretty little maids

Below: The dancers from Scottish Ballet welcome their patron, Princess Margaret

Above: Prince Charles meets well-wishers
at the Royal Gala Opening in 1982

Left: The Earl of Wessex unveils the bust
of Frank Matcham

The Spirit of the Show

From the 1920s onward – there's always been a Show:
That tradition drives us onward, urging us to – Go! Go! Go!

The stirring 'Finale Chorus', written in the 1950s by George Low with music by Reg Barrett-Ayres, encapsulates the whole spirit of the charity *Student Shows*. Founded with a mock trial in the University Debating Chamber in 1921, the annual *Student Show* has grown over the ensuing years in its irreverence to local characters, businesses and local politics and nurtured an audience who love every minute of its catchy tunes, witty songs, clever scripts and storylines.

It began as a contribution to the broader charities campaign to raise funds for Aberdeen hospitals and now collects enormous sums of money for a wide range of charities across north-east Scotland, laying waste the myth of the meanness of Aberdonians. The show played many venues across the city, including the Aberdeen College Hall and the Palace Theatre, before finding its real home at His Majesty's Theatre in 1929. It occasionally moved to the Beach Pavilion, Hilton College and the Music Hall when the theatre was out of commission.

Stars born in *Student Shows* include, in the early years, Eric Linklater, Sonia Dresdel, Andrew Cruickshank, Stephen Mitchell and Moultrie Kelsall. More recent performers, familiar to the present generation of Aberdeen audiences, give an indication of the wealth of talent within our city. The author has opted for those he knew and worked with and apologises for omissions due to memory failure – Barry Symes, Buff and Margaret Hardie, Stephen and Eva Robertson, Douglas Kynoch, George and Sheila Reid, Derek Brechin, Harry Hill, Ian Middler, Roddy Begg, Jill Hay, June Imray, Ruth Nicol Smith, Charles and Margo Barron, Donald Manson, Larry Gray, Quentin Cramb, Ronnie Middleton, David and Gwen Haggart, John Hardie and Craig Pike.

1958   1959   1963

Above and right: Programmes for *Student Shows* over the years

The same applies to the author's recollections of the unsung stars of the *Student Show*: energetic, hard-working producers – Reg Barrett-Ayres, Bill Ramsay, George Low, Alan Nicol and James Logan; backstage heroes – Bill McCann, George Sinclair, Colin Mackenzie, Derek Nisbet, Sandy Youngson, John Webster and Gus Law; dancing queens – Eileen Ewen and Jean Birse; talented scenic artists – Alex Young and Melvin Dalgarno; make-up artists – George Grant and Sandy Dale; ladies of the Wardrobe – Alice Sparke (who dressed a whole show in 1943 with only ten clothing coupons) and Ena McLaughlan; and, finally, the administrators (who are almost always forgotten but carry the whole responsibility for putting the show together) – business entrepreneurs Philip Ross, Robin McLeod, Bob Downie, John Bain, Alec Main and John Duffus.

The *Student Show* has rung the changes over the years, swinging from revue performances to musical comedies, from specially written music to reworkings of current hit tunes, from original scripts to parodies of West End musicals and television shows and, in so doing, has remained fresh in its appeal to its loyal and supportive audience.

1970

1995

1996

2000

The Financial Crisis

The Donalds kept His Majesty's going for several decades on a fairly sound financial basis, bringing a wealth of talent to Aberdeen and filling in the 'dark' weeks with film screenings or variety performances. But, in the 1960s, they began to feel the effects of rising costs, particularly those of transport.

His Majesty's was still independent of any local authority funding and was then the only major theatre in Scotland to operate without it. The first approach for financial support was made to Aberdeen Town Council in 1966 for a production of *Peter Pan* and a Gilbert and Sullivan operetta to be presented by the D'Oyly Carte Opera Company. The council granted £1,000 and this was increased the following year to £6,000, with a further grant of £3,500 in 1969. It was becoming increasingly clear that, if the theatre was to continue bringing high-quality artistic productions to the city, a much more permanent arrangement had to be reached.

James F.

Factors within the Donald organisation brought matters to a head. In 1971, General Manager James R. Donald, who was also a highly respected Dean of Guild in the city, passed away and was succeeded by his eldest son, James Forrest Donald. Although he continued the tradition of courtesy and charm for which the family was known, he instituted changes to put the theatre on a better financial footing. He ended the arrangement with Howard & Wyndam – under which they handled all bookings for His Majesty's for a hefty commission – and undertook bookings himself, stamping his personality on all future programmes. Booking at least a year ahead, he skilfully judged the tastes of his patrons and brought the very best entertainment to the city. However, despite good houses and reasonable returns, the costs of running His Majesty's continued to rise.

Finally, external events brought a resolution. The gaming company Ladbrokes made an offer in 1973 to buy the company James F. Donald (Aberdeen Cinemas) in order to acquire His Majesty's as a possible casino. Rather than lose its theatrical heritage, the Donald family offered it to Aberdeen Town Council for the bargain price of £350,000. With a grant of £100,000 from the Scottish Arts Council, the council was able to accept the offer on 5 September 1974 – and wisely invited James F. Donald to continue as director, assisted by his brother Peter as manager.

This arrangement took the theatre through many successful and exciting years until 1983, when changes in the J. F. Donald Organisation led to Mr Richard Donald taking over sole control and the organisation's association with His Majesty's ended after fifty years. James then entered into a ten-year contract with the council to direct the day-to-day running of His Majesty's, with all other staff directly employed by the council. This he fulfilled, retiring in 1994, and, although Peter continued for a further four years as manager, direction and control passed to other hands.

Peter B.

Looking back on his career, James had much to be proud of but perhaps his greatest pleasure came from the extensive refurbishment, carried out between 1980 and 1982, and the formation of the Theatre Club. This allowed members to enjoy discounts, priority booking, after-show parties and lunchtime talks, in exchange for an annual subscription. The financial success that followed made His Majesty's Theatre one of the most successful in the country. Audiences responded to the attractions in his carefully balanced programme and the box office did record business.

Uniforms through the years

From the 1930s until 1980, staff wore adapted cinema
uniforms until specially designed ones appeared from
1982 onwards

The front of house foreman felt the cold in the foyer
so he wore brown paper wrapped round his legs –
he was known as 'The Rustler'!

The doorman wore a bright red coat

The usherettes must have melted under these heavy dresses

1970s – still cinema-style uniforms
but in a lighter material

The bright and cheerful uniforms from the 1980s with very frilly, feminine costumes for the ladies

John Brand, front of house supervisor, assisted by Iain Stewart, parades the staff in their new uniforms for 2005

George 'Dod' Hay

The Interval

Characters from Behind the Safety Curtain

Rude Mechanicals

For many in the theatre industry, baring your soul on stage as an actor or singer is neither fulfilling nor satisfying. A whole different life exists behind the house tabs (the main curtain at the front of the stage) – a life that is varied in its opportunities for expression and unforgiving in its demands for skills and which can provide rich pickings for legends of successes and disasters. 'Rude mechanicals' have their own folklore, their own ethics and every one is a character.

George 'Dod' Hay
The man behind 12,000 shows

Born in 1878, George served his apprenticeship as a blacksmith, also finding time to be an all-round sportsman. He excelled at football, playing a full season in 1908 with Aberdeen Football Club. He was employed by Robert Arthur as a blacksmith on 18 July 1910, just four years after His Majesty's opened. During the First World War, he was seconded back to heavy industry with the Henderson Engineering Company. On his return to the theatre, he was advised to give up heavy work and became a flyman, working in the fly tower above the stage. This seemed to be a strange decision, considering the hard work involved in operating a hemp rope flying system.

With the sale of the theatre to Walter S. Gilbert in 1923, George was appointed resident stage manager, a post he held until 1950. However he continued working for a few more years as the theatre handyman.

His greatest legacy is his immaculately kept ledger of the flying plot of every show he worked on. Written in elegant copperplate, it provides today's researcher with a detailed record of the rich and varied programme presented during those early years. It confirms, for example, that it was normal for the O'Mara Opera Company to perform six operas in one week and for the Henry Baynton and Sir Frank Benson Companies to present nine and six Shakespeare plays respectively during their one-week visits.

The book notes the first performance in Scotland of Puccini's opera *Turandot* by the Covent Garden Opera Company, on 4 October 1929, and records for posterity appearances by Sir Harry Lauder, Harry Gordon, Wee Georgie Wood and a host of other variety stars. It also shows that, although the revolving stage was installed by James F. Donald in August 1933 and was used initially for *Evenings of Pictures and Variety*, its first use for a pure stage show was on 25 September that year for the first visit of *White Horse Inn*.

During the Depression of the early 1930s, when work was scarce, a line of some fifty men would queue up on a Monday morning at the Stage Door. George Hay – in suit, bowler hat and watch chain – would parade along the row to select his staff for the week, favouring those he knew had families to feed. In the same attire, he took up station in the Prompt Corner for the run of the show, controlling his staff with a quiet word or a stern reprimand.

He was a stage manager of the old school and his craft skills are still evident in

This fly book was meticulously written up by the Resident Stage Manager, George Hay.

The wind machine   The heavy rain machine

the theatre. Clamps, large chisels, hammers and three-foot-long screwdrivers for removing seats – all handmade and stamped with his name – are still in use. Visiting school parties are always intrigued by the original sound effects machines – the wind machine, the thunder sheet, devices to mimic a seashore, falling rain, a pistol shot or a slap to the face – and all are testament to the ingenuity of this first real resident stage manager at His Majesty's Theatre, who oversaw some 12,000 shows during his working life.

During the refurbishment of 2003–05, scenery and props were removed to storage around the city and, unfortunately, some of the items created by George Hay were misplaced. Hopefully these will reappear in the course of time and resume their role as part of the fascinating heritage of His Majesty's Theatre.

Bert Ewen

George Hay was succeeded by Hebbie Silver, a Mr Walsh, a Mr Thomson, Ronnie Mackie and a Mr Robson albeit for short periods of service – Robson lasted just a few weeks. The Donald Family needed a stage manager they could trust to maintain the high standards of His Majesty's. They had such a man in the chief projectionist at their other variety theatre, the Capitol Cinema, which also featured the Donald programming policy of pictures and variety. Albert Ewen, known to all as Bert, came to His Majesty's in the summer of 1956 and stayed until 1979, quickly establishing himself very much as a hands-on manager.

Bert Ewen

He was a popular figure who made friends easily with visiting performers and technical crews and his own staff, particularly young students looking for part-time work. Generous with his philosophy on life and show business in particular, he could be quite scathing with those who did not come up to standard. If he had a fault, it was that he was accident-prone, probably as a result of his desire to be involved in the physical side of his duties. He was once hoisted fifteen feet in the air with a snap hook through his hand, when he criticised the fly floor crew for being too slow to respond to his shout to 'take it away'.

Bert operated an open house in his tiny stage manager's office on the back stairs, every Friday after the show. A cup of tea – and more often something stronger – would accompany his stories about shows and show people, which were rich entertainment in their own right. Critiques of artistes were offered – many complimentary, some unprintable but all most entertaining.

He also had a stock of wartime recollections. He had served in the Home Guard during the Second World War, in a unit formed to accommodate workers in the

The two pals at Bert's retirement party (Bert Ewen and George Sinclair)

cinema and theatre industries. Sunday was their only day off and they spent it training – which, according to Bert, usually consisted of a game of football down on the Beach Links. One day, the unit was ordered to defend the Woolmanhill Drill Hall, behind His Majesty's Theatre, against a raid by a squad of Canadian commandos training for a future raid on Dieppe. Perhaps it wasn't surprising that the attack lasted just three minutes before the projectionists and stage crew surrendered. There were no hard feelings – they and their colonial cousins retired to the nearest pub to celebrate!

It was at one of Bert's soirees, after *An Evening with Hinge and Bracket*, that a casual conversation led to the author giving up his teaching career to become the theatre's first technical director. He had a good staff around him, all imbued with an old-fashioned dedication and giving their best to ensure a smooth-running show. His staff book for 1957, in which he recorded information for the wages bill, lists the following: in the flies, Minty, Cassie, Aitken Sr, Aitken Jr, Hall and Webster; on props, Slater, Cocker and Singer; on stage, on Opposite Prompt side, Hannah, Irvine, Reith and Whyte; and, on the Prompt Side, Mackie, Fraser, Gray and Punt. Many of the staff were firemen on time off or bakers on night shift from Mitchell and Muill's bakery. One staff member, Charlie Craig, was janitor at Robert Gordon's College.

George Sinclair

Bert was always particularly helpful to the local amateur companies and his great sparring partner in these was George Sinclair, stage manager for the *Eileen Ewen Shows*, the Lyric Musical Society and the *Student Shows*. Although they were the very best of friends, no quarter was given in any discussion about how many staff were needed for each show or whether scenery should be flown in from the fly tower above or run on to the stage from the wings at the same level.

George Sinclair

George was a teacher by profession and he rose to the post of headmaster at Powis Academy. He first became involved in the theatre when he did National Service as a 'Bevan Boy' in the coal mines near Newcastle. On his return to Aberdeen, he staged many shows at His Majesty's – thirty-eight *Student Shows*, thirty-two for the Lyric, four for Eileen Ewen and three for Powis Academy. He eventually retired through ill health. For all his association with show business, he was still unable to render any song in tune, as he used to demonstrate at after-show parties with an excruciating version of 'Honeysuckle Rose'.

His great pride was the *Student Shows'* stock of scenery, which he guarded and maintained in farm buildings belonging to the university at Balgownie. At one time, it was a better stock than held by many professional theatres. Sadly, after his retirement, vandalism led to the building becoming less than wind and watertight and the stock of flats, rostra, backcloths, props and costumes was destroyed.

Dougie Monaghan

Now and again in the life of theatre, one comes across a true gentleman and this is an apt description of Douglas Monaghan. He began his career in the theatre in 1938, as a pageboy fetching taxis from as far as the Victoria Park, jumping on the dashboard for the journey back to the front door ready for the patron and then dashing off to fetch the next one. He recalls that, until the last patron cleared the foyer, the front-of-house staff remained at attention at their posts.

He progressed to train as a projectionist and, when he returned after war service in the Royal Navy, he succeeded Harry Weberley as chief electrician, recording at his retirement some fifty-one years of service to His Majesty's. His commitment to the job is legendary. Stories are told that he would go home and – becoming uncertain whether he had switched off equipment or locked up properly – would return in the small hours to make sure the building was secure. He had a particular duty of care for

Dougie Monaghan discusses his Royal Navy days with HRH Prince Charles

the younger members of his staff, fussing over them and their work to ensure his pride in the job was instilled in them.

In his time, he witnessed the replacement of the Strand Electric Grand Master lighting controller. Built like the bridge of a ship, complete with polished brass rails, it occupied the whole of the Prompt Corner but it was replaced by a small,

The Strand Electric Grand Master – built like the bridge of a ship

computerised desk sitting at the back of the Stalls. Sound amplification devices also changed, from cumbersome stand mikes and hand-helds to miniature radio mikes concealed in the hairline.

All this Dougie took with a wry smile and good humour, encouraging his younger staff to take advantage of the advances in technology. His successor, George Thompson, eventually moved south to Glasgow, to become lighting designer with Scottish Ballet.

The present chief electrician, Kay Donaldson, is the first woman to hold this post at His Majesty's and she is also building a strong reputation as a scenic designer and artist.

Stage and Technical Managers

Bert Ewen retired before the refurbishment of the theatre in 1980. He was succeeded by Douglas Shepherd who, at the time of his appointment, was the youngest resident stage manager in a major British theatre. Doug enhanced the theatre's reputation for well-run backstage facilities, which may help explain why many companies with the prospect of only one Scottish date chose His Majesty's. He developed a flair for stage design that was put to excellent use for the home-produced Scottish variety shows, which brought good returns at this time. But he took ill before his full potential could be realised and died very young.

His successor, John Hyde Kerr, came from the Belfast Opera House and reigned briefly at His Majesty's before returning to his native city. The post then went to Doug's brother Graeme who had years of experience as a stagehand and was multi-talented in the skills needed for modern scenery construction. He has guided the backstage crew through their recent decanting to Hilton College and the return to a completely refurbished stage after the 2003–05 rebuild. The new technical manager Sandy McRobbie has carried responsibility for the transition since his move to the post, direct from the Millennium Dome in London.

Doug Shepherd – the youngest resident stage manager

Stage crew in 1980 drinking the bar dry before the theatre closed for refurbishment

The 2005 crew – Spike, Paul, Graeme, Greig, Keith and Kay

Mr Music Man

Dressing Room One was the happy home for many years of the charismatic musical director, Lambert Wilson. The cupboards were packed with orchestrations for every conceivable theatrical occasion, whether it was for the variety presentations that formed part of the *Evenings of Pictures and Variety* – when he and his orchestra were swung round to entertain for the second part of the evening – or to provide the interval music with his trio for the seasons of repertory theatre. Saturday matinees often involved a hasty dash from Isaac Benzie's tearoom in George Street, where he also entertained.

A remarkably fit man, famous for making a record-breaking swim from the Dee to the Don, he moved to Bournemouth to continue playing and teaching until his death in 1996 – at the same age as his beloved His Majesty's Theatre.

Lambert Wilson – 'Mr Music Man'

Lad o' Parts

Bill Cassie was a big strong man – which was ideal for his duties as a part-time flyman – but he was a man of many parts. He was the shop steward for NATKE, the stagehands' union, but he was also an expert on Billy Bunter and a lover of light opera. He would debate nightly on politics, religion, art and music and he loved strong tea. Dod Slater, the head props man, met his need by filling the large kettle on Monday, throwing in a handful of tea and sitting it on the gas ring. Each succeeding evening another handful of tea was added until second house Saturday, when the beverage was of the perfect consistency for sizing canvas and Bill loved it!

Bob Singer, props man on the Opposite Prompt side, always insisted that new staff should cover one eye before a blackout scene change (and they were real blackouts in those days before health and safety considerations introduced the soft blue lighting that is favoured today) so that at least one eye would be adjusted to the darkness. That was until one night during panto season, when he rushed in, caught his neck on Wishee Washee's clothesline and brought scenery tumbling down across the stage! Those of us new to the game at the time often wondered if this was part of the induction procedure – similar to being sent for a left-handed screwdriver or a tin of tartan paint!

Up until the 1940s, there was a backstage beer bar for stage crew, members of the band and visiting artistes. When this was closed, the Well o' Spa Bar across the road at the back of the theatre fulfilled the role. Not the most salubrious of drinking establishments, it nevertheless performed miracles every interval, pulling the fastest pints in the business. During variety weeks, first-act performers often had to be fetched from the pub to do their walkdown for the finale. During one Saturday matinee performance of *Snow White and the Seven Dwarfs*, only two of the

Well o' Spa Bar, until its demolition, the 'refreshment room' for staff, musicians and artistes

little people made it on to the stage. The rest had to be fetched by the front-of-house foreman Norman Robertson from various bushes in the Union Terrace Gardens and carried back to their dressing rooms to be sobered up for the evening performance!

The closure of the Spa Bar, to make way for the Denburn Health Centre, coincided with the end of a Saturday performance by Scottish Opera. 'Scottie' McLaughlan, the well-known city lawyer and financial manager for the *Eileen Ewen Shows*, organised a wonderful farewell for the Spa. Artistes, members of the orchestra, theatre staff and amateur 'luvvies' gathered at 10.30 p.m. to drink it dry and strip it bare of any souvenir that could be kept as a memory of this most popular part of life backstage at His Majesty's.

Long Service

His Majesty's Theatre has always had staff who have given long and dedicated service. In the 1980s, a public enquiry into an accident at the theatre was held before the sheriff in Aberdeen's courthouse. It was quite revealing as witnesses from the part-time day staff gave their ages – seventy-eight, eighty, sixty-nine, etc. Gladys Bicocchi was reluctantly retired as coffee lady in her eighties – with never a cup lost nor a shortage in the cash box! Norman Robertson, front-of-house foreman; Alec Carr, senior usher; May Fraser, Dress Circle Bar staff; Pat Tough, Stalls Bar staff; Mary Taylor, secretary to the director; Anne Russell, Theatre Club secretary; Lynne Greig, wardrobe mistress; Ina

Mary Taylor, secretary to the director, James F. Donald

Watt and Georgie Sinclair from the box office – all of these were long-serving members of the staff His Majesty's.

Pat Ross, long-serving fireman and later Stage Doorman, was friend to all at the back door, always courteous and patient with cast reluctant to return to their digs. He had one encounter with an international star, which has become part of the folklore. It was at a time when there was a problem with 'dossers' and 'winos' in the park at the rear of the theatre. Pat's instructions were to be extra vigilant with strangers at the door. This he duly did when the famous French jazz violinist Stéphane Grappelli arrived late in the evening for an after-show performance. Pat took one look at this figure in a raincoat and beret, speaking in a language Pat couldn't understand, and promptly threw him out! Poor Grappelli had to make his way round to the front door to plead for admission.

Pat Ross – a most conscientious stage doorman

Sheila Macdonald, who recently retired as senior usherette, has a few tales to tell. One concerns an inebriated lady patron who visited the ladies' toilet during a ballet performance, dropped her trousers and fell down the back of the toilet. She was trapped there, with her body on one side and her knickers and trousers on the other, until Sheila clambered over the dividing partition to effect an embarrassing rescue. On another occasion, a gentleman was ejected for stealing pre-poured drinks in the Stalls Bar. He was out on the street before the staff noticed he had no shoes. Onstage, a dark and creepy play was being performed and Sheila brought many a scream as she crawled in to recover the shoes!

Front of house manager, Norman Robertson, parades the staff before opening up the doors

The cold and scary Lambeth Walk leading from the Balcony along the back of the Fly Floor down to the church lane

Jake the Ghost

A theatre is ideal for a ghost. It is a place where the imagination is stretched. Like a giant battery, it has years of aesthetic energy stored within its walls. Reality has to be suspended in the theatre and every one has its own superstitions, alongside universal taboos such as whistling backstage or mentioning the title of Shakespeare's Scottish play. When you mix imagination and superstition in the same pot, it is not surprising that apparitions and hauntings materialise. Every theatre worth its salt has to have at least one ghost. Roy Harley Lewis's book *Theatre Ghosts* lists the spectral residents of theatres from Drury Lane in London to Eden Court in Inverness, calling in at Aberdeen on the way.

His Majesty's Theatre is blessed with Jake, a harmless apparition, mischievous rather than scary, but his existence requires some explanation. Before the 1980–82 refurbishment, the backstage area had a hemp flying system containing some six miles of Manila hemp rope, a wooden grid and fly floor. Weather conditions, particularly heavy wind and rain, produced creaks and groans and the banging of shutters and doors – rather similar to the sounds of a fully rigged sailing ship. Rather than waste time and effort investigating these strange noises, it was much easier to blame them on Jake. Similarly, if a screwdriver went astray and then turned up the next day, Jake was the culprit.

There was a factual reason for naming him Jake. In 1942, a circus was performing at the theatre. Horses were to be brought up to the stage by means of a hand-wound stage hoist. One night, the lift was overloaded and proved too much for the men winding the winch in the basement. John 'Jake' Murray leaned over to apply the brake and was decapitated by the spinning winch-handle. As the sightings and weird noises began to mount, a charisma was bestowed on the ghost far above his original persona. He was 'seen' on the bridge to the fly floor. He was 'heard' to walk on Lambeth Walk, the long passage running from the Balcony to the internal fire escape stairs.

During the 1980–82 building works, Taylor Woodrow, the contractor, hired a nightwatchman to guard valuable equipment. He had an Alsatian guard dog called Savage, who did an excellent job patrolling the building until he came to Lambeth Walk. On arriving there, he would perch on his haunches and lay his ears back with his fur bristling. Savage was not the only one to perceive something odd in that part of the theatre. Despite central heating, there are occasions when, with no rational cause, the temperature along the Walk will drop to near freezing.

When working alone through the night, the author had some strange experiences while painting scenery on the paint frame high above the stage. While drawing was carried out on the scenery flats, paintbrushes would be laid by the sink. Minutes later, they would be found on the windowsill or the work table, several feet away. Perhaps tiredness was leading to memory lapses so particular note was taken of where the brush was left yet still it was moved. Only a shout of, 'Jake! Leave my brushes alone!' would put a stop to the mischief.

On other occasions, the author was grateful for Jake's assistance. In the small hours one morning, he fell down some stairs and, convinced he had broken his ankle, crawled his way down to the basement, heading for the accident and emergency unit, which was then based at nearby Woolmanhill Hospital. That night, he found the padlock on the Dock Door open and the chain hanging loose. This made the journey across the road much easier than usual and the badly sprained ankle was treated. Bert Ewen swore the next day that he had left the door secure.

Another night, while working on stage with the safety curtain up, the author had a problem with the nozzle of a can of gold spray paint. Frustrated and weary, he stuck a pin in the hole and the can exploded in his face, blinding him. He knew he had to get to the Props Room sink to wash his eyes out. He had lost all sense of direction and could easily have gone over the footlights and into the orchestra pit, perhaps with tragic results; but something took control of his actions and, within seconds, he found himself at the sink. Thanks, Jake!

Pete Thorpe, who was resident stage manager at His Majesty's briefly before he joined Scottish Opera, was a sceptic regarding ghosts but he did admit to two strange experiences. On one occasion, he heard footsteps on the fly floor when he knew there was nobody else in the building. Another time, he met a figure in a brown dustcoat, on the bridge behind the paint frame, who disappeared before his very eyes.

There might also be a second ghost. Two young artistes appearing at His Majesty's once asked Dougie Monaghan whether the theatre was haunted. They described in great detail an old lady they had seen walking through the Stalls Bar and, as Doug listened, he realised they were exactly describing Miss Mitchell, who had worked in that bar for a long time but had died some years previously.

After the 1980–82 refurbishment, when wood and rope was replaced with steel and wire, the strange noises disappeared. Perhaps Jake and Miss Mitchell are taking a rest until the opportunity arises, some time in the future, to come back to life.

Loads of Fun

Often, hilarious incidents occur backstage to which the audience is oblivious but which make for great entertainment when recounted in the Props Room during the morning tea break.

At the end of one performance, Pip Floyd Murphy of Scottish Opera had his arm through the handle on the back of the house curtain, ready to make a cave to allow the principals to go through to take their footlight bows. The girl on the desk in the Prompt Corner leaned forward to get a better view and accidentally pushed the go button for the fly floor. Away went the curtain with Pip clinging on for dear life. His wife, playing in the orchestra, saw a pair of feet below the curtain and, recognising his pink socks, screamed, 'That's my Pip!'

Another time, during a *Five Past Eight* show, there was a scene change for a Rikki Fulton kitchen sketch. In the blackout, little Dougie Whyte accidentally placed weights on the skirt of a black tab curtain, pinning it down. When the cue was given to fly the tabs out, six men in the flys pulled with all their might – whereupon the tabs ripped right across the top hem and fell away. Suddenly much lighter, the fly bar holding the curtain shot up to the grid and six men landed in a heap on the fly floor, losing their grip on the ropes. The fly bar crashed back down to the stage just as the revolve was turning and it swept the set into the wings with a resounding crash. It was pushed back on to the revolve, which continued to turn as the front tabs were opened. But the set was now in the wrong position – its side flats were caught by the tabs and the whole thing toppled like a pack of cards. Lighting operators on a bridge above the stage collapsed in laughter as chaos reigned. The audience appeared to take it all in their stride – perhaps they assumed it was all part of the Scottish variety scene!

A Birthday Whirl

Jenny Shirreffs

Jenny Shirreffs, a stalwart worker for His Majesty's, was accorded the honour of having her birthday party on the stage. It was a wonderful evening, with lots of food served in the theatre bars and then everyone gathered on the stage for an evening of dancing. The band was set up at the back of the revolve and the bandleader announced the first dance – a Gay Gordons. The music struck up, the dancers danced and the next minute the revolve sprang into action! The band, their music stands, microphones, sound equipment, cables and all the dancers set off on a mad whirl.

Doug Shepherd, the stage manager, rushed forward and jammed a crowbar into the edge of the revolve and brought the chaos to a halt. The revolve sits freely on the stage, its own weight keeping it stationary, but the vibration caused by the enthusiasm of the dancers proved to be too much and it had decided to join in the fun. Metal plates were quickly screwed down and the evening's entertainment continued and was enjoyed by all. Certainly a birthday to remember!

Swans A-Swimming

One Friday evening, after a performance by London City Ballet, guests at a sponsor's after-show party were invited by a very senior member of management to visit the backstage area. The safety curtain was raised so that the full glory of the auditorium could be admired. The fun started when the manager pressed what he thought was the button to lower the curtain. Within seconds, the stage was flooded by the emergency sprinkler system. In an attempt to turn off the deluge, he hit

another button and the pressure pumps came on, increasing the flow to a torrent.

Meanwhile, the resident and visiting crews were enjoying a small libation in a nearby pub. On hearing the fire brigade's sirens, they rushed back to the theatre to assist in the clear-up operation. With their help – and the stalwart efforts of the city's finest – the flood was swept from the stage, out of the orchestra pit, from the mezzanine floor, down the dressing room stairs and into the basement and cellar, from where it was pumped out on to the street. With the help of the police, the owner of a gas tank supply depot was awakened about 2 a.m. and large gas tanks were dispatched for the theatre's blow-heaters. These were directed on to the back of the house tabs to dry them out.

By 10 a.m., when the ballet chorus were due on stage for class, the building was completely dried out and there was no evidence of the near-disaster. The identity of the very senior manager is a theatrical secret but the biggest laugh about the whole incident still remains – the show to be performed that night was *Swan Lake*!

The paint frame in 1932, showing the
mixing palette table and the hand winch
used by the Small Family

The paint frame in 1982, now powered
by a powerful electric motor

Stars of the Paint Frame

In many top-class theatres, the facilities for scenery construction and painting are in buildings separate from the theatre. His Majesty's is one of only a few where there are workshops in the basement and a splendid paint frame some thirty feet above the stage.

However, the frame's position has presented some special problems over the years. In the days when it was raised and lowered by a hand winch, it could not be used during rehearsals or shows. During the preparations for the Whatmore Players' first production in 1956, Jean Anderson, the assistant scenic artist, broke her arm on the winch. The author, then a student at Gray's School of Art, was sent along for a week to fill in. He remained there until he retired in 1993.

Extra care had also to be taken when cooking the size, which was used for binding the scenic powder colours to the canvas. If it was overheated, the burnt smell permeated right through to the back of the Stalls. Sizing new fireproofed canvas also released the wonderful smell of rotten eggs! On many an occasion during the repertory seasons, the theatre staff has to resort to the famous Donald spray guns to mask the revolting smell!

The paint frame's original floorboards, dating from 1906, were cracked and split and leaked like a sieve. If a bucket of paint was knocked over, it spelled disaster for anyone or anything on the stage below. Eileen Ewen, an elegant and gracious lady, who was loved and respected for the dancing shows she presented over many years at the theatre, was an unfortunate victim of the author's carelessness. Minutes before she made her final curtain call at the end of a show, her beautiful cocktail dress was splattered with spilled paint. She had to rush back to her dressing room and change into the clothes she had worn to come to the theatre. The author had to make a shamefaced apology and was graciously forgiven.

On another occasion, when art student Alex Young and the author were painting during the night, a bucket was knocked over and a gallon of white paint poured over the red velvet upholstered seats of a suite of Jacobean furniture being used in a play. Panic produced the answer to the disaster! A sharp knife was used to remove all the covers. They were washed in the Props Room sink and placed over the huge stage radiators to dry and in the early morning they were stapled back in place. No one was any the wiser.

Eileen Ewen

Scenery by John Whiton Small, who resided at 38 South Constitution Street, painted for Her Majesty's Opera House before he moved to His Majesty's Theatre

The Scouts' *Gang Show* also suffered. A sailing ship, lovingly created by designer Alan Ritchie, fell victim to yet another knocked-over bucket. The beautiful sails appeared on stage not so much as 'Red Sails in the Sunset' but a deep shade of green!

Since 1906, many artists have worked on the paint frame, producing colourful backdrops. Sadly many of their names have been lost in the mists of time. However, people still remember the Small Family. William Whiton Small was the scenic artist at the Queen's Theatre, Dublin, for twenty-seven years and was succeeded at that theatre by his son Robert. Another son, John Whiton Small, worked for many years at the Britannia Theatre in Hoxton, London before being appointed to Her Majesty's (now the Tivoli), Aberdeen, in September 1890, at a salary of three pounds a week.

He moved to His Majesty's when it opened in 1906 and served the theatre for some thirty-five years. His backdrops were wonderful paintings, forty feet by twenty-four feet, and many are preserved on the racks in the theatre's cellar. One of the best known is the Loch Lomond set, with a realistic moon ripple effect. During the theatre's eightieth anniversary celebrations, one of his

The snow scene painted by the Smalls for His Majesty's Theatre.
A stock backcloth, it was used in several shows

Anastasia

The Hasty Heart

Bell, Book and Candle

Arsenic and Old Lace

Scenery by Ani Jasper for The Whatmore Players

cloths was displayed to great acclaim in the courtyard of Aberdeen Art Gallery. A highly regarded painter in oils, John Small exhibited regularly at the Royal Academy in Edinburgh and the Aberdeen Artists' Society.

On John's passing in 1938, he was succeeded by his son, Leo Small, who painted for the Tivoli and His Majesty's. He was a fast worker – on one occasion, he painted ten complete sets, including the wings, in just three weeks. Leo was a well-known character in Aberdeen. A highly regarded lithographic etcher, he ran a scenery and lighting hire business from a draughty wooden store in East North Street, next to the Model Lodging House. His and his father's surviving works were identified recently, by experts from the Theatre Trust, as treasures of the utmost national importance.

The visit of the Whatmore Players repertory company in 1956 brought these scenic skills back to the forefront. Normally, rep companies toured with their sets but, on this occasion, it was decided that the sets for the twelve-week season would be created in-house. Ani Jasper, a top-class designer straight from London's West End, was engaged and soon enthralled Aberdeen audiences with the stunning beauty of her sets. It became quite normal for her set to receive a round of applause as soon as the house tabs were raised and before a word was spoken. The modern practice, by which sets are seen by the audience as soon as they enter the auditorium, means that scenic artists are denied this acclaim.

Ani Jasper married Shelley Masters in Aberdeen and she moved on to new ventures, to be succeeded by Sheila Ward and Nevil Dicken, who maintained the high standard for Dennis Ramsden's productions for the Whatmore Players. The heyday of Scottish variety shows – such as the *Stanley Baxter Shows* and the *Five Past Eight* productions – brought with it the stunning sets of Reg Allan from Howard & Wyndham's Glasgow workshops.

Local artists have always been encouraged to make use of the paint frame. It is hoped that, with the new developments in the theatre's educational programme, many local artists will grab the opportunity to explore this wonderful craft.

Alan Ritchie will be long remembered for his clever constructions to accommodate the cast of hundreds in the Scouts' *Gang Shows* and the Grampian Education Authority production of *A Note of Class*. Moira Greig did beautifully decorative sets for Aberdeen Opera Company. Well-known local artist Eric Auld did two sets for the Lyric Musical Society – *Night in Venice* and *Showboat*. Like his more familiar public work, they were outstanding in colour and decoration. The complete sets for the highly successful Andy Stewart seasons, the *Jim MacLeod*

Set for *Camelot* by Jane Ancona and Susan Ball

Shows, *Scotland The What?* and the *Fiddlers' Spectaculars* were all created in-house.

In the late 1980s, the partnership of Jane Ancona and Susan Ball produced work at the theatre for various local productions. Jane came with a vast experience in theatre work, particularly at the Gaiety Theatre in Ayr. Susan originally studied sculpture at Wolverhampton College of Art and Gray's School of Art in Aberdeen and she and Jane worked together for many years until Jane retired and moved south. Susan continued to work alone and produced memorable sets for many venues, including His Majesty's, with productions ranging from *Jesus Christ Superstar* to Benjamin Britten's opera *Peter Grimes*.

Sets by Susan Bell

The Pirates of Penzance

Carousel

Copacabana

Sets for *The Caucasian Chalk Circle* by The Studio Theatre Group

The author made full use of the revolving stage to provide the range of scene changes required for this production – it also used up all the scrap timber lying in the cellar!

Jack Pirrie

The theatre's signwriter, Jack Pirrie, carried out his first commission for His Majesty's in 1938. This was a standing cut-out for *Emile Zola*. Thereafter, he produced, by hand, the weekly bills for the theatre display cases, the huge advertising hoarding that used to be displayed on the back of the theatre and the thirty-six-foot-long banner above the front entrance. Paper shortages during the war years forced Jack to utilise the backs of old posters.

Jack Pirrie – Grand Old Man of Lettering

Originally one of the best-known screen-printers and signwriters in Aberdeen, he trained many young apprentices in his time and, on his retirement from business in 1983, he again undertook to produce the large bills that graced the front of the theatre every week. His skill for freehand drawn lettering is exceptional – and it's remarkable that his eye is still as good and his hand still rock steady at the age of ninety.

With the 2005 refurbishment now complete, Jack has taken the opportunity to retire and put his brushes to rest. His contribution to the life of His Majesty's Theatre has been recognised by the theatre management, who have dedicated a seat in the auditorium in his honour.

The Theatre Chaplain

This book is dedicated to the memory of Dean Campbell Adamson, chaplain to His Majesty's Theatre from 1970 until his death in 1983. He was a very special person, fulfilling a very personal role backstage as the theatre's representative of the Actors'

Church Union (ACU). His detailed research into the history of Aberdeen's theatre was the inspiration for this book.

The ACU was formed by a London clergyman, Donald Hole, to meet the needs of theatrical personnel who, by nature of their way of life, were travelling on Sundays and so were unable to attend churches and maintain the practice of their faith. Wherever in the world there is an English-speaking theatre, there is an honorary chaplain. He or she can be found in theatres, in radio and television studios, in stage schools and ballet schools and at RADA. Overseas, ACU chaplains can be found in such diverse locations as Beirut, Boston, Hollywood, Toronto, Las Vegas, Paris and Monte Carlo, offering spiritual and moral welfare or simply fellowship to artistes and technicians. At one time, there were in excess of 700 chaplains but, with the demise of many provincial theatres, they now number about 200.

Despite the onerous demands on him as a parish priest, Campbell always found time to be around on an opening day, when he would visit the dressing rooms and give a smiling welcome. Offers of a tour of the city or a run up Deeside, followed by tea at the vestry, were welcomed and long-lasting friendships were established with big stars and lowly members of the chorus. He was particularly friendly with the resident crew, who regarded him as one of their pals. The serious side of his duties he carried out with great sincerity and discretion.

The present chaplain is Rev. Emsley Nimmo of St Margaret's Scottish Episcopal Church in the Gallowgate. He is ideally suited to carry on the work of the ACU, being a singer and musician of some standing in the city.

High Jinks at Nannie Martin's

In Back Wynd, above what used to be a grocer's shop on the corner of Schoolhill, stood the famous theatrical digs run by Nannie Martin. These were particularly popular with comedians, dancers and stage crews working in variety shows at the Tivoli and His Majesty's. Nannie was extremely tolerant of the high spirits of her guests and suffered, in the nicest possible way, the pranks they played on her.

During an Andy Stewart summer season, her guests included dancer Dixie Ingram, entertainer Sydney Devine, company manager Russell Lane and stage manager Roy Devrill. They had a great affection for Nannie but that did not stop them carrying out the most outrageous prank of all. One afternoon, Sydney pretended that the door of his room upstairs had jammed. Feigning claustrophobia, he yelled to Nannie to let him out. As hard as she pushed against the door, Syd held it firm. Thus distracted, she was unaware that, in the meantime, the rest of the rogues had removed every item of furniture from her room – her bed, dining table and chairs, cupboards, wardrobes, radio and television set – and arranged them outside along the pavement in Back Wynd. Eventually Syd released the door, thanked Nannie profusely for saving him from his worst fears and brought her downstairs to reveal a totally gutted house!

Her initial dismay and panic turned to roars of laughter when she was eventually taken outside to find that a fair-sized crowd had gathered, under the illusion the house was on fire! The household goods were duly returned. All was forgiven and tiny little Nannie cooked her guests a lovely tea before they made their way to His Majesty's for the evening performance.

High spirits occasionally surfaced at the theatre during a performance. Andy Stewart had a very funny sketch in which he portrayed the old guide in a Scottish castle. The set consisted of a wall in the main hall of the castle, adorned with a huge picture frame covered with a curtain. Andy would stop the tour party at the picture and draw back the curtain to reveal Dixie Ingram – who incidentally was Andy's brother-in-law – frozen in a pose as Bonnie Prince Charlie. Andy would then crack a few gags to make Dixie laugh, whereupon he would deliver the tag line, 'Sorry, that wasn't Bonnie Prince Charlie – that was the Laughing Cavalier!' Shut curtain! Blackout!

Very funny. Until the night when Andy drew back the curtain and there was Dixie not as Bonnie Prince Charlie but on his knees as Toulouse-Lautrec, the short-legged French artist! All Andy could do was stare in disbelief, mouth open, then close the curtain and go straight to the blackout! The rest of the company, who had been pre-warned, were doubled up with fits of laughter at the back of the Stalls and the Dress Circle.

The Best Story of All

There are many contenders for the best theatrical anecdote but high on the list must be the story retold by Scottish actor John Shedden at a party in his home town of Lerwick, Shetland, concerning the famous Shakespearean actor Sir Donald Wolfitt. He was a regular and popular visitor to Aberdeen so this apocryphal story could have happened at His Majesty's.

At the end of an exhausting performance, Wolfitt was prone to stagger downstage, lean against the proscenium and, with a hand mopping his brow, give out advance notice of the following week's presentation. He announced that it would be a performance of the *Scottish Play* and that he, of course, would be playing Macbeth and that his beautiful wife Rosalind would be playing Lady Macbeth. A shout from the Balcony challenged the purity of Rosalind's morals, 'Ah! Your wife's a . . .!'

'Nevertheless,' retorted Wolfitt, 'she will be playing Lady Macbeth!'

The traditional hemp rope flying system
could not cope with modern technical demands

No more brute strength!

Act Two

The Story Continues under Aberdeen Town Council Control

Failed by the Act

Under local authority ownership but with the expertise of the Donald Family controlling programming and finance – a unique arrangement in Scotland – His Majesty's Theatre confounded all the critics by becoming the most successful civic theatre in the country. In the first six months, an estimated loss of £150,000 was converted into a profit of £35,000. In the words of the hit musical *Gypsy*, 'Everything was coming up roses'. But then the Health and Safety Act (1974) raised its ugly head and presented the local authority with a dilemma. One of their best-loved buildings was in urgent need of surgery if they were to implement the Act and preserve its existence. The council recognised the importance of a first-class theatre, presenting the very best of large-scale entertainment, as an essential element in their provision of a vibrant cultural, educational and recreational policy.

Six and a half miles of Manila hemp rope

Exemptions to the Act were granted until the council committed themselves to an act of faith in 1979, at a time of severe financial restraint, to allocate £3 million to meet the demands of that Act.

The paint frame counterweights –
colourful but dangerous!

Because of the problems with the Denburn River
the whole basement had to be redesigned

The open-sided lift shaft
presented major problems

The old advertiser cloth occupied a valuable
set of lines in front of the house tabs

Changes Are Made

Although the theatre was adored by its citizens, it failed to satisfy the new health and safety regulations in many areas. The stage hoist, essential for bringing scenery up on stage from the basement storage area, had open sides and was moved by an unsafe mechanism. It had to be totally enclosed in a shaft, be powered by screw-jack lifting gear and be equipped with extensive fail-safe devices.

In order to meet the demands of touring companies, the existing flying system, with its six miles of Manila hemp rope, had to go. It was the last of its kind in a major British theatre and relied for its efficiency on sheer brute strength of sometimes up to twenty stagehands, aided by a precarious arrangement of sandbags and heavy steel weights clamped to the ropes. It could only have remained in service if all actors, singers and dancers wore safety helmets! A new counterweight flying system was proposed, incorporating an eighteen-tonne grid, supported on four steel legs, rising from the basement to the roof. One of these legs landed on top of the culvert carrying the Denburn, which runs under the theatre. Sixteen feet wide and seven feet deep, it lay only inches below the basement floor. A reinforced concrete bridge had to be built over the river, which raised the basement floor level and led to a complete redesign of the whole area.

The paint frame was also declared illegal under the Act. Its hand-wound winch and its counterweights – which hung on exposed wires – were deemed unsafe and were to be replaced by a steel frame, raised and lowered by powerful motors installed in the roof.

The management also recognised the rapid advancement in theatre technology in the provision of lighting and sound amplification. A new control room was created at the rear of the Upper Circle and in this air-conditioned suite sits the most sophisticated computer equipment available at the time. A vast array of powerful

The new eighteen-tonne grid
is ready for lifting – the first time
this has been attempted

The new all-steel fly floor is in position

The new counterweight flying system

Clockwise from above:

The new orchestra pit

The redesigned basement with the new enclosed lift shaft

Johnny Robertson checks the new colour scheme for the ceiling

The new advertiser is painted on the new safety curtain – the work of Chris Clark, one of the country's finest scenic artists

The auditorium glowing with Peter Rice's new colour scheme

The Dress Circle Bar with the first
art exhibition by artist Frank Stephen

lights was tucked under the Balcony and ranked in tiers above and at the sides of
the stage area. Considering that each of the 200-odd lamps is as powerful as a two-
bar electric fire, the electricity board showed good sense by installing a new sub-
station at the rear of St Mark's Church.

In any theatre refurbishment, it is important that the acting area and its related
technical equipment should receive priority, allowing the finest plays, the most
complicated musicals and operas and the most beautifully staged ballets to be
performed. The quality of the performance on stage is what entices the audience
and puts bums on seats.

But the patrons' comfort is also important. Peter Rice, the eminent theatre
designer, was engaged. He produced a rich and sumptuous colour scheme, with
excellent use of 24-carat gold leaf to pick out detail in the auditorium and Dress
Circle Bar. He produced designs for new wallpapers, carpets and curtains,
replacement house tabs, the advertising display on the safety curtain and a new
chandelier. All the seats were re-padded and repositioned to give more legroom and
remove forever the former problem of the pillar seats in the Back Stalls.

The new house border and new chandelier

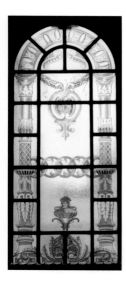

Restored
stained glass
window in
the foyer

An enlarged, sunken orchestra pit allowed large orchestras for opera and ballet performances to be accommodated well below sightline, without impairing sound quality. New gas central heating and ventilation, allied with a total smoking ban in the auditorium, ensured an improved atmosphere. Provision for disabled patrons was given special priority, with the addition of a ramp entrance from the Church Lane, a free seating area and an inductive loop for the hard of hearing.

His Majesty's Theatre closed on Saturday, 4 October 1980 with a performance of *The Pirates of Penzance* by the D'Oyly Carte Opera Company – the first opera company to appear at the theatre after its acquisition by J. F. Donald in 1933. Backstage staff, scenery and lighting equipment moved to the former Corporation Works Department in Jasmine Terrace. Front-of-house staff moved to the Capitol and some shows were presented there during the two-year closure, including two pantomimes, one of which was presented by the local Attic Theatre Company, produced by that great lady of the local theatre scene, Annie Inglis.

The project was led by the city architect Ian Ferguson and his project manager Bill Moir and the building contract was awarded to Taylor Woodrow Construction (Scotland). Under the direction of Marcus Freckingham, assisted by John Burgis, planning engineer, it was completed on time and within budget. This success was due in no small way to the effort of the subcontractors, who were hassled and cajoled by the site foreman Johnny Robertson, who never stopped running for two years!

There was friendly co-operation between the theatre management and the theatrical consultants from John Wycham Associates, Tony Easterbrook and Len Greenwood. Tony became very fond of Aberdeen on his visits. He was very partial to an Aberdeen 'rowie' and never set off for the airport without a visit to Stephen Wilson, the bakers on Skene Square, for his fortnightly supply!

There were many moments between October 1980 and September 1982 when the destruction and chaos made one wonder if the theatre would ever come alive again. At 7 p.m. on the opening night of the trial show, the week before the official opening, the performance licence was finally granted. It had been delayed because of loose carpet fittings at the Stalls doors out into the lane. The curtain rose on *The King and I*, presented by the pupils of Powis Academy. The performers, the staff backstage and front-of-house and all the new equipment came through that baptism of fire bathed in glory.

However, it was not to last. When His Royal Highness the Prince of Wales stepped out on stage on 17 September 1982 to declare His Majesty's Theatre well and truly open, the riser mike, which was normally operated by a pulley system from the Prompt Corner, jammed solid and had to be pushed up by hand from below. The prince was greatly amused to look down and see a face looking straight up his kilt! That royal gala opening show, *Curtain Up*, revealed some other snags. The safety devices on the stage hoist kept getting confused signals and cutting out the motors. Then, the shaft of the screw-jacks had to be turned by hand, by anybody who was available. Ian Eccles, the city council's lift engineer, lived in the theatre for the entire week! On the Friday evening, there was a strong wind and heavy rain poured down on to the stage through a broken hatch on the roof – the ventriloquist Roger De Courcey

The programme from *Curtain Up*, the royal gala opening show, 1982

A revenue flyer

His Majesty's Theatre
Aberdeen
"BRITAIN'S MOST BEAUTIFUL"

FRANK MATCHAM 1906

THE FIGURES SPEAK FOR THEMSELVES!

NOV 1987 REBECCA STORM
EVITA *3 weeks*
£200,676

DEC 1987 Bill Owen Paul Henry
CINDERELLA *4 weeks*
£207,875

JAN 1988 SCOTTISH BALLET
The Nutcracker *1 week*
£47,201

JAN 1988
ROWAN ATKINSON *4 perfs*
£48,381

FEB 1988 Lulu & George Cole
PETER PAN *2 weeks*
£121,736

FEB 1988 A Man for All Seasons
CHARLTON HESTON *1 week*
£93,048

WHY NOT SHARE IN OUR CONTINUING SUCCESS?

Enquiries, for bookings from March 1989 onwards, to -
JAMES F DONALD *Theatre Director*
HIS MAJESTY'S THEATRE *Rosemount Viaduct*
ABERDEEN AB9 1GL *Telephone* 0224 637788

wished he had brought an umbrella for his friend Nookie Bear. The author spent the evening lying on the roof, dressed in his dinner suit, holding down a sheet of plastic in an attempt to stem the flow. He arrived at the after-show reception soaked to the skin!

There was one other unfortunate accident during the *Curtain Up* show. A young member of the ballet chorus stumbled, due to a discrepancy between the level of the revolving stage and the surrounding stage area and broke her leg, which adversely affected her career.

Many of the restorations carried out during this refurbishment were highly innovative. The redesign of the lettering above the front facade – which now read simply 'HIS MAJESTY'S' – was considered for a Civic Award. The replacement of some 200 panes of stained glass – achieved with the help of two lecturers from Gray's School of Art, Ian Pirie and John Smith – was received with great acclaim. One part of the process was completely unique. The new grid, built by the local firm Bon Accord Construction, was delivered in sections, re-assembled on stage and raised into position fifty feet above the stage in one piece. It was the first time this operation had been carried out in a British theatre and was made possible by spin-off technology originally developed for the offshore oil industry.

The council soon realised that their investment was

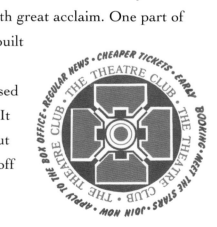

A Theatre Club beer mat

Smashing records at Scottish jewel

ABERDEEN'S HIS MAJESTY'S Theatre, splendidly refurbished at a cost of £3,500,000 two years ago, is proving the jewel in the crown of Scotland's theatres.

The municipally-owned theatre has been smashing box office records since it reopened with the consistency of a Coe or an Ovett.

Recently the ridiculously cramped box office took more than £10,000 worth of bookings in one day.

Prompting the merry ring of cash tills were three shows – Scotland The What, the Paul Daniels' Show and the pantomime "Aladdin."

And the accounts for the six months up to the end of September reveal that the theatre has turned an expected £25,000 deficit into a profit of £78,240.

"It's been a smashing six months. We took over half a million pounds in box office receipts during the period," announced theatre director James Donald.

And what is delighting him even more is that the best months have now arrived. Summer, with the long daylight hours, is usually the theatre's low season.

The "Northern Lights" are certainly shining bright over one particular piece of Aberdeen real estate.

A clip from *The Stage and Television Today*

James's booking plan

a sound one. Audience figures zoomed to dizzy heights and His Majesty's very quickly established itself as the most successful provincial theatre in the country. The City Chamberlain's Department had estimated that the theatre would lose £148,000 in the first six months after refurbishment but enthusiastic support from the citizens of Aberdeen and the surrounding area turned that into a profit of £84,000. The success was not temporary. Year after year, the box office returns made many provincial theatre managers green with envy – and some in the West End of London.

A great contribution to the financial success was the establishment of the Theatre Club. Anne Russell ran this organisation and her informative and chatty newsletters soon established a rapport with the members. Membership rose to over 4,000 private and a considerable number of corporate members. Each newsletter had the box office tills struggling to cope with the demand for tickets. The privilege of being member number one was accorded to Graeme Wilson, a well-known supporter of the arts in the city.

The success of His Majesty's caught the attention of the managers of touring companies and they were soon knocking at James Donald's door looking for bookings. In this climate, he could afford to be selective. His booking plans reveal how the programme for the forthcoming year was balanced. There was something for everyone. Prestigious, high-quality shows for the ballet and opera lover, popular plays featuring familiar stars from the small screen, large-scale hit musicals, something for the children and, now and then, the occasional risqué presentation for the more adult patron.

One show can claim universal appeal and it commands a very special place in the story of His Majesty's Theatre. Three men with a piano and a wealth of talent created a legend.

No, not the Three Tenors –
but the Three Managers from
1982, painted by Eric Auld

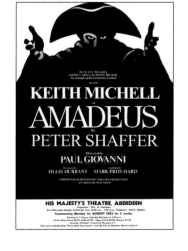

Stephen Robertson, George Donald, Buff Hardie and James Logan

Scotland the What?

James Logan, the meticulous producer of *Scotland the What?*, always insisted on the question mark. It grew from a ditty, 'Some say Scotland the brave but we say Scotland the what?' and it was very largely due to his attention to detail that the performances came across as very relaxed and casual. If a sketch didn't have six good laughs, it was out and James never allowed the 'boys' to move more than three feet from a microphone. They accepted this firm control thanks to a friendship that was established over their collective apprenticeship in becoming the funniest, most polished act to hit the Scottish variety entertainment scene.

Buff Hardie and Stephen Robertson first met in the *Student Shows* of the 1950s and, although George Donald contributed material to the 1954 *Student Show*, the link with him and James Logan was made in the Aberdeen Revue Group. This group featured some of the most talented entertainers in the city – among them, Anne Brand, Quentin Cramb, Margaret Hardie, Rose McBain, George Reid, Derek Brechin, Alfie Wood, Pat Wood and Douglas Kynoch. It was the birthplace of kernels of ideas that went on to be developed into the classic sketches that made *Scotland the What?* such a success. So much of their dialogue has become part of the Aberdeen local patois: ''At's an affa lot a' toilet rolls in yer basket – is a'body fine?'; 'Is 'at a Baxi?'; 'Is 'at Co-opie coal?' 'We dinna buy Co-opie coal – it's ower weet!'; 'He's in Forrresterrrhill – wi a'body roon aboot his bed.'; 'Wis his funeral in cinema one or cinema two?'

Pressure from family and business commitments led to the wind-up of Aberdeen Revue Group with *Going, Going* . . . at the Arts Centre in 1967. Buff Hardie, Stephen Robertson and George Donald, along with James Logan as producer, the refugees from the Revue Group, put their considerable talents together to form *Scotland the What?* Visits to the Edinburgh Festival in 1969 and 1970 drew much acclaim and the attention of James F. Donald who offered the group a booking for a Friday and Saturday in 1971. Such was the reception that an extra performance on the Sunday was hastily arranged. Bookings then followed every two years at His Majesty's, with visits to theatres across Scotland and notable performances in London – at the Duke of York Theatre in 1975, the Queen Elizabeth Hall in 1985 and the Bloomsbury Theatre in 1987. In 1988, *Scotland the What?* came to the rescue at His Majesty's by performing for six weeks, living in the band room while the dressing rooms were completely refurbished.

In 1993, James Logan retired and Alan Franchi, a highly respected television producer, took over the reins for tours until *The Final Fling* at His Majesty's in 1995, the 'mop-up' show which drew *Scotland the What?* to a close. George still continues to tour with his own show, Steve is now director of the Deeside Festival (which brought all three together again for an onstage chat show in 2005) and Buff has

been known to come out of retirement on occasion, to give hilarious after-dinner speeches.

The 'boys' are regarded with great affection and respect throughout north-east Scotland. This fact was acknowledged by their alma mater on 26 November 1994 when, along with their mentor James F. Donald, the University of Aberdeen accorded them Honorary Degrees of Masters of the University. Their standing as consummate entertainers throughout the country was recognised the following year when they received MBEs from Her Majesty the Queen.

Although no longer performing as a team, they leave behind, on audio- and videotape, wonderful memories of three men in dinner suits who brought so much joy and laughter to our lives.

The End of an Era

In that same year of 1994, James F. Donald completed his contract with Aberdeen City Council and retired, to spend more time with his wife Anne and their family – and to improve his skill on the golf course. Thus the direction of the theatre by the Donald Family came to an end – although it should be noted that James's younger brother Peter continued as theatre manager for another four years, retiring in June 1998.

For one family to be associated with the successful management of such an enterprise for such a long time must be unique in the annals of British theatre history.

Peter's retirement brought an end to the Donald Dynasty

Robert Robson

Robert Robson took over at His Majesty's Theatre with a firm commitment to revitalise the role of the theatre in the cultural life of the city. He came from a background of community drama in Glasgow, then spent seven years as artistic director of the Cumbernauld Theatre and four years as director of Glasgow's prestigious Mayfest. His policy envisaged radical changes to programming, moves to attract a younger audience and structural changes to the building, including new rehearsal and catering facilities to permit its broader use.

Robert Robson

He was resolute in his determination to implement his vision for the theatre and unfortunately some of his plans did not sit well with his patrons – especially when comments he made in private in a bid to stimulate debate were leaked, out of context, to a wider audience.

In September 1998, after four years in the post, Robert resigned to take up a post as theatres director at the £127 million Lowry Centre at Salford in Lancashire. When this prestigious arts complex opened in 2000, he was responsible for programming its two theatre spaces. In 2003, he was promoted to become the centre's overall artistic director.

The debate on the future of His Majesty's and how it could best meet the needs of its audience was now firmly in the public sector. All concerned recognised that the search for a new director should be extensive and thorough.

Theatre boss criticised over comments

A THEATRE boss who criticised his audiences for living in an artistic backwater has come under fire from his critics.

Mr Robert Robson, of His Majesty's Theatre, in Aberdeen, described the city as unenlightened and unsophisticated.

In a report to Aberdeen City Council he said that any native with talent should quickly get out of the city. And he said Scotland the What? and radio presenter Robbie Shepherd

were two of the "downsides" of Aberdeen.

Mr Edi Swan, former artistic director at the theatre, said that he could not go along with Mr Robson's view that the city was not artistic. "Some of the work that is done by amateur companies in Aberdeen is of the highest standard," he said.

Mr Robbie Shepherd, whose radio programme is one of the most popular produced by BBC Scotland, was also critical.

He said: "If Mr Robson

wants to make his theatre elitist then it's a sorry day for the city's traditional entertainers. What he seems to forget is that 'Scotland the What?' repeatedly filled that theatre of his for entire summer seasons."

The theatre boss, who also has responsibility for other venues in the city, including the Music Hall and Arts Centre, made his outspoken comments in a confidential report to Mr Brian Woodcock, the council's director of arts and recreation.

In the document Mr Robson said Aberdonians were narrow-minded, inward-looking and mean-spirited. He pointed out that Aberdeen produces less plays than Perth which is smaller and claims it has produced few actors, musicians or writers of note.

"This paper is written not out of personal frustration but from a deep sense of disbelief at how unenlightened and unsophisticated a city Aberdeen would appear to be," he said.

Theatre boss hits out at claim

by **Ken Banks**

THE boss of Aberdeen's HM Theatre has hit out at reports that he painted a cruel image of the city in a leaked report.

Robert Robson apologised for any offence that may have been caused — but said his comments had been taken out of context from a dated confidential document.

HMT director Mr Robson was reported in a Sunday newspaper to have described Aberdonians as being

unsophisticated and narrow-minded.

The internal document had been prepared for the city's arts and recreation department.

Mayfest

Mr Robson said last night he could not really comment on any leaked information but added that the report in question was around six months old. He went on: "Words were taken out of context but if any offence was caused I am sorry for that."

Mr Robson, a leading figure in the Scottish theatre world, took up his current post in 1994, after a spell as director of Glasgow's internationally-renowned Mayfest.

He took over the helm from James Donald, who retired after a lifetime at the theatre.

Mr Robson said on his appointment that he wanted to attract a younger audience with international work, comedy, contemporary dance and music programmes — without alienating loyal theatregoers.

■ **Robert Robson**
. . . leaked document

Aberdeen anger

Aberdonians have reacted angrily to claims by the director of the city's leading theatre that they are "narrow minded, inward-looking and mean-spirited", *writes Hamish Mackay.*

In a leaked local authority report, Robert Robson, who has run His Majesty's in Aberdeen since 1994, also claimed that some of the best performers born in the city, including singer Annie Lennox and dancer Michael Clark, had left it at the earliest opportunity.

"Style, creativity, flair and imagination are not qualities

that are valued in Aberdeen and often construed as arrogance," he stated. "Someone has to question the city's complacency."

And his criticism of leading popular local performers, BBC broadcaster Robbie Shepherd and the highly popular Scotland the What revue trio, brought a stinging rebuke from Shepherd. "If he ever said this in public, he would have to resign," he said.

However, Robson declared he had no intention of resigning, saying his comments were confidential and had been taken out of context. "What I am trying to say is we do need to expand our programme. We have a problem with programming and what is available across Britain."

HM Theatre programme

SIR, — The council's proposal of a major development for HM Theatre, Aberdeen, is interesting in itself, but it raises a serious question of artistic priorities.

Speaking as one who has been a member of the Theatre Club since it began, I am profoundly disappointed at the deterioration in the theatre's programme over the last few years — an almost unrelieved sequence of musicals, mostly of the rock and jazz variety, and hit plays from the London circuit, with a very occasional visit from Scottish Opera or Scottish Ballet. The Aberdeen theatregoing public deserves, and I am sure wants, better treatment than this.

Not only do we get virtually no quality drama, we get virtually nothing of Scottish, much less North-eastern, interest. For all the awareness shown by the HM Theatre management that it is serving a community with a strong sense of local cultural identity, the theatre might as well be in London, Leeds or Land's End. This is nothing less than a total dereliction of artistic responsibility.

And while the council is considering spending an enormous sum on the upgrading of a theatre with no artistic policy worth mentioning, we are told that it can't afford to maintain the Arts Centre, which makes a vital and irreplaceable contribution to the artistic and cultural life of Aberdeen and the Northeast.

A theatre which has no better idea of its function and responsibility than to pursue a crude "bums on seats" policy by presenting a lot of vacuous rubbish does not deserve massive subsidies from the public coffers. One which encourages serious and interesting drama, gives support to Scottish and regional culture and provides a venue for the community's lively amateur theatrical scene most certainly does.

1994

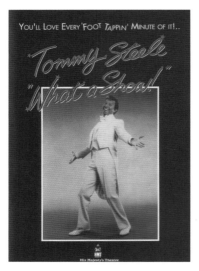

1994

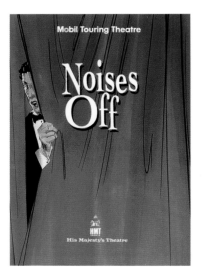

1995

1995

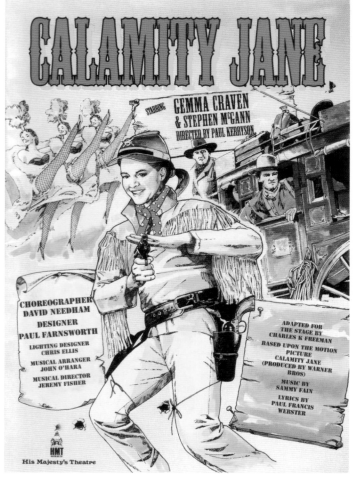

1996

1996

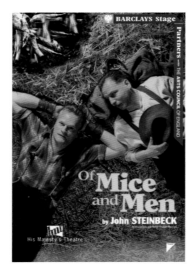

1996

1997

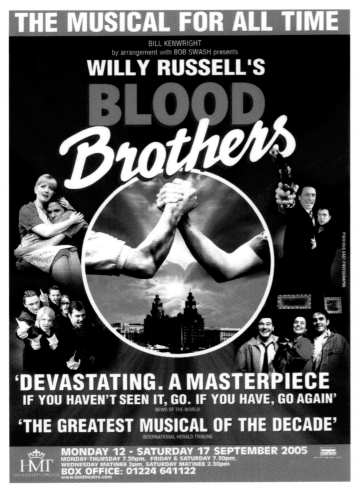

1997

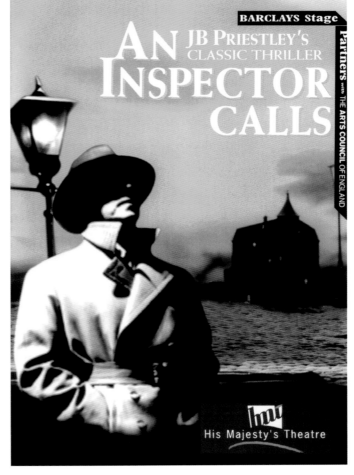

1999

Duncan Hendry

After completing a degree in psychology at St Andrews University, Duncan joined Unicorn Leisure in Glasgow and then moved to be their General Manager in Edinburgh. He came to Aberdeen in 1975, delved briefly into pub ownership and then developed his career in artist management and concert promotion.

Duncan Hendry

In 1988, he became director of the Aberdeen Alternative Festival, a post he held for ten years. Duncan brought star names from the world of jazz and contemporary music to the Festival, many of whom appeared at His Majesty's. Stéphane Grappelli, Emmylou Harris, Elvis Costello and Michael Nyman were just a few of the international stars presented at HMT by the Alternative Festival whilst James Brown, Van Morrison and Art Blakey were among a host of stars who performed at the Music Hall and Aberdeen Exhibition Centre during his spell as Festival Director. This was Duncan's first involvement in programming work into His Majesty's but this experience in the early to mid 1990s and the close working relationship established with the then theatre director, James Donald, were to stand him in good stead in the years to come.

Duncan was appointed operations manager at the Music Hall and, following Robert Robson's departure, he became general manager of both the Music Hall and His Majesty's Theatre in 1999.

The following year, Aberdeen City Council instigated changes in the way the theatre was to be owned and managed with the formation of the Aberdeen Performing Arts Trust and, in 2000, Duncan Hendry was appointed its first general manager. Changes had been mooted which proposed organising the city into three areas – North, Central and South – each with its own administrative body. It was felt that sport and cultural activity would be best served if these were controlled by arm's-length organisations. On 9 March 2000, Councillor David Clyne moved:

> [In] order to get the best value for the people of Aberdeen from the revenue budget and to attract outside funding for the provision of . . . cultural facilities in the city . . . the Council, without commitment, investigates the setting-up of a cultural trust for the performing arts, encompassing all the Council's performing arts facilities.

During the following year, a working group assessed all the implications of the proposed move. Several meetings and presentations took place investigating the role of the trust and issues concerning legalities, finance and personnel. In November 2001, a transitional board was formed, with Councillor Clyne as its chairman, and it presented its action plan in March 2002. After due deliberation by the Council, it was approved and, on 1 April 2004, Aberdeen Performing Arts Trust took over control of His Majesty's Theatre, The Music Hall and Aberdeen Box Office. It was incorporated in November 2002 as a non-profit-making distributing company with limited liability and charitable status.

The trust's board includes fifteen members – seven are City Councillors and the remainder are residents of the city with expertise in business, education, marketing and public relations. With two venues and the box office now under its control, the trust needed to make radical changes to staffing, financial control and programming. The faith placed in Duncan by the board was recognised when he was promoted in 2005 to the post of chief executive.

Duncan's policy is simple and straightforward. It is to provide the very highest quality of entertainment in both venues under his control. To do this, he has instigated and overseen improvements to provide the finest buildings to house that entertainment, to appoint the best-qualified people to staff these venues and to set up a structure that enhances fast and appropriate decision-making. Both venues and the box office already contribute greatly to the cultural life of the city. In terms of returns on investment, it also brings considerable financial gains. Over 100 people are in employment and the annual turnover is in excess of £5 million. It is estimated that, in return for an annual investment of approximately £1 million by the local authority, over £20 million is generated in income for the city. The popularity of theatrical entertainment must never be underestimated. It is a fact that more people visit His Majesty's than attend Pittodrie Stadium for home games!

His Majesty's is destined to be more than a receiving theatre. The National Theatre of Scotland is booked to rehearse and perform a new stage version of John Byrne's hit television series *Tutti Frutti* from the new rehearsal premises. Other new productions, particularly those that encompass the culture of north-east Scotland, are in the pipeline. Local amateurs can rehearse in the wonderful new facilities at a cost no greater than what they currently pay at local churches and schools. A youth theatre now meets every Saturday morning. The restaurant and coffee shop are open all day. Changes are already in place – changes which Duncan Hendry sees as establishing His Majesty's Theatre as a major creative force in the city.

Members of the Board of the Aberdeen Performing Arts Trust
Back row: Mr Charles Kelly, Councillor Ronald Webster, Mr Ken McLeod, Chief Executive
Duncan Hendry, Dr Graeme Roberts, Mr Neil Jones, Mr Buff Hardie, Councillor John Stewart
Front row: Councillor John Porter, Councillor Karen Shirron, Ms Morag Pyper,
Mrs Jenny Shirreffs, Mrs Dawn Eunson, Councillor George Adam
Not Pictured: Councillor Neil Fletcher, Councillor Karen Freel

Moving Out
The Hilton Experience

Before any rebuilding could be started, a new home had to be found for His Majesty's Theatre. A survey was carried out at the Tivoli Theatre on Guild Street to ascertain its suitability but it soon became clear that the costs to bring it up to usable standards and comply with all the current health and safety and disabled access regulations would be prohibitive. An estimate of £1.7 million was put forward, which was too high even to be considered. This obviously was a disappointment to the Tivoli Trust, which had hoped that this would be a first step in its own restoration.

An alternative was found at the former Aberdeen College of Education Assembly Hall on the campus at Hilton. Now owned by the University of Aberdeen, this building was due for demolition once its new Education Department was completed at King Street.

It was an appropriate choice. It was blessed with good car parking, it had modern toilet facilities in reasonable condition and adequate office space close at hand. However, despite its close association with James Scotland, the playwright and producer who, as head of the college, insisted on its inclusion in the building plans and although it was well used by the staff of the college's drama department – including Annie Inglis, Alan Nicol, Ron Sawden and Charles Barron – it had limitations for modern large-scale professional productions.

The seats were better suited for short assemblies, there was no emergency lighting and the sound and lighting provision was below acceptable standards. The control box dominated the centre of the auditorium, there were no follow-spot positions, no talkback provision, no flying grid and the acoustics needed to be dampened.

A twelve-week period was allocated to deal with these problems. Sandy McRobbie was designated as project manager and, with the able assistance of Graeme Shepherd, Kay Donaldson, Brian Dempster and the resident crew of His Majesty's, he achieved the impossible. All was ready for the opening show, presented by Scottish Opera.

Carpeting was laid and 320 seats from the Stalls at His Majesty's were installed in the lower area to give more comfortable seating. Trusses were slung from the roof to support front-of-house lighting. A new control box and positions for follow spots were built at the rear of the hall and many metres of blue drapes were purchased and hung over the windows and side walls to dampen the acoustics and provide an ambience more suitable for performances

Existing facilities in the hall were adapted to create a bar, coffee shop, sales area and box office. Rooms were refurbished to provide dressing rooms, toilets, showers, a wardrobe and a green room for visiting artistes. These arrangements kept the site compact and secure without the need to resort, as was first feared, to ancillary accommodation in Portakabins.

Scenery and lighting equipment not required at Hilton were stored at an industrial estate at Dyce – this included the collection of historically important backcloths. Alterations to the basement area at His Majesty's Theatre have resulted in a smaller storage area for scenery and the Dyce store will be kept until a decision is made over what is to be returned to the theatre.

The hall in its college days

HMT at Hilton
open for business

In store at Dyce

Work in progress

A taste of the varied
programme presented at Hilton

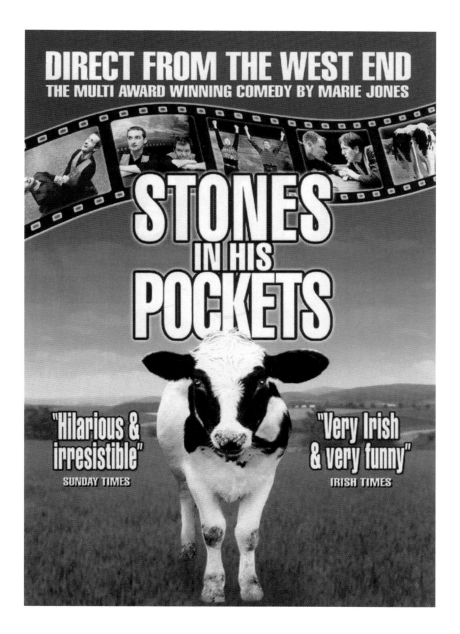

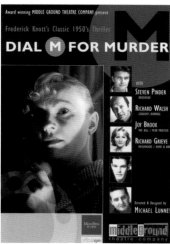

The move to Hilton also presented other problems. Careful consideration had to be given to the types of productions that could be staged, given the limitations of the venue. Duncan Hendry sought out producers and production companies that could fit the bill. They, of course, were quite different from his normal contacts when filling the larger venue at His Majesty's. The success of his endeavours can be measured by the post-mortem on the Hilton exercise.

Theatrical entertainment was kept alive. The Theatre Club membership was retained throughout the period. Essential backstage and front-of-house staff, vital to the ongoing life of the theatre, were kept in continuous employment – important for their years of service benefits. Despite all the difficulties, almost 60,000 patrons enjoyed the very best quality of shows that could be presented. In particular, the Christmas pantomime, *Snow White and the Seven Dwarfs*, did very good business – although it attracted some controversy over some children who were deemed to be unsuitable to appear in the show. The *Student Show* and the local group Flying Pigs enjoyed virtual sell-outs. However, it was with great relief that everyone, staff and patrons alike, made the return to their proper home on Rosemount Viaduct on 8 September 2005.

The Need for Refurbishment

Despite valiant efforts over the years to keep His Majesty's abreast of current legislation, two problems had needed urgent attention.

Toilet provision in His Majesty's was never fully satisfactory. Extra ladies' toilets were added in 1985 in the basement area but these were underused because of their location and were inaccessible to the less able. Other toilets were upgraded where possible, with modern plumbing substituted for leaking urinals and lead pipework. Elsewhere, where repair was impossible, toilets were boarded up. The provision of hot water frequently relied on ingenuity – often with cosmetically unsatisfactory outcomes. Queuing, especially for the ladies', became an irritant on what should have been a pleasurable night out. It was recognised that these failings presented a threat for the renewal of the theatre's licence.

The frieze close up

The Disability Discrimination Acts of 2004 and 2005 again highlighted the problem of access to toilets and also access to the stage, dressing rooms and parts of the auditorium other than the Stalls, where access was available for wheelchair-users via a ramp from Church Lane (now named Donald's Way). The Dress Circle was the only other area accessible to patrons with limited mobility – although, even here, steps at the front door had to be negotiated first.

Consideration of these problems very quickly revealed that a new build had to be considered, adjacent to the existing theatre. The creation of lift shafts, for example, meant losing toilet space and, without major alterations to Matcham's concept, that toilet space could not be replaced. There were also other important questions to be resolved.

His Majesty' Theatre was only open to the public during performances. When not open for that purpose, it was a gloomy building whose doors were locked for most of the day. It was a building that was underused. Its potential to play an important role in the cultural life of the city was not being fully exploited. It needed a restaurant and coffee shop, an in-house booking office and a rehearsal area at least as large as the stage to allow for the development of in-house productions. In the past, when sponsorship functions were held in the Dress Circle Bar, ordinary patrons were prevented from using it. A separate corporate hospitality area was needed. The new educational programme – which had been planned to enhance participants' experience of the theatre – called for additional staff and accommodation. Further expansion in staffing to increase returns from sponsorship, promotion and ancillary trading called for improved office space and access to that space.

His Majesty's also had a duty of care to its performers and technicians. Improvements had been made to the stage, stage hoist, paint frame and flying system during the 1980–82 refurbishment and to the dressing rooms in 1988 but technology always advances ahead of its provision. Upgrades to lighting and sound and an overhaul of the stage hoist to meet current health and safety regulations were deemed necessary. A green room where cast and crew could meet, relax and socialise – which is standard in most theatres – had never been available at the theatre and its provision would be welcomed by visiting shows.

All this had to be provided within an extension that also had to be energy-efficient, environmentally friendly, open and welcoming, particularly to a younger audience. It should be built in good quality, modern materials sympathetic to (but not imitating) the existing structure and within an affordable budget. Had the new extension been built on a different site within the city, it would have been a straightforward construction project. However, it had to be built in the former car park at the side of the theatre and access had to be created through the gable end of the theatre – made from thousands of tons of Tillyfourie granite – to provide links to the existing parts of the building.

As was the case in the 1980–82 reconstruction, the Denburn was also a problem. After emerging from under the basement, it then meanders across the car park. Test pits had to be dug to confirm its path. These confirmed that, three metres down, under sand and gravel, there was solid granite bedrock. Concrete rings were sunk through the topsoil. These were then filled and they carry the whole weight of the extension away from the Denburn culvert. The steel framework of the new extension is therefore a free-standing structure, independent of the existing

Matcham building and Rosemount Viaduct, which runs along its frontage.

Where the Denburn passed under the gable, the whole weight of the wall was carried by the huge original girder, that had been inserted when the theatre was built and which spans the culvert at ground level. To have broken out numerous openings without extra support would have put the whole structure at risk. A massive steel truss was placed temporarily on the inside, at ground level, to carry support beams until the openings were completed. Fifteen of these were required to create doorways and ducts at all levels, the largest being the wide corridor running from the new foyer through to the old foyer and the Dress Circle. A new archway was created, where the small door from the old foyer to the Balcony was situated. Again this involved temporary bracing until the archway was completed.

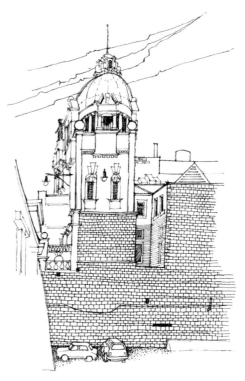

The gable end carrying thousands of tons of granite

Differences in floor levels meant removing and reconstructing the stairway tower under the dome, from ground level to the fifth floor. This was a difficult undertaking, which required the demolition of stairs within a tower that carried the weight not only of the dome but also of the large water storage tank inside it.

The task of designing the project was placed in the capable hands of Trevor Smith from the city's architects department, who had already achieved award-winning success with his design for the Aberdeen Maritime Museum. He recognised from the outset that to attach an extension to the side of the existing building in the same architectural style would disrupt the elegant, carefully

The huge truss in the basement

Breaking through the internal walls

considered balance of Matcham's original design. To do so would be a desecration. It would also have been financially prohibitive. And, perhaps most important of all, it would have failed to meet essential elements of the design rationale – the newbuild was required to be open and welcoming, attractive to a younger audience, energy-efficient and environmentally friendly.

Trevor set out to create a building that was sympathetic to the Matcham design but one that would also stand in its own right as a piece of contemporary architecture. Like its neighbour, it would be constructed using the finest materials available. The craftsmanship, as in 1906, would be of the highest order to ensure low maintenance and a sustainable future, at least on a par with the original building.

The contract was awarded to local firm the Robertson Construction Group, with David Steel as project manager. He recalls that there were unique problems. The building was a warren of corridors, staircases and rooms and it was initially quite easy to get confused and lost. The site was very constricted, limited in storage space and manoeuvrability. Steel beams weighing over one tonne could not be slung in with a crane. They had to be carried and positioned manually and, because of that, the project was very labour-intensive. During the course of the project, the workforce rose to almost 700.

Backstage in the old theatre, the theatrical consultants Carr and Angier recommended that the revolving stage had outlived its usefulness and should be removed and that the distance between the fly floors should be increased to permit a forty-foot width for flown scenery. Karen Dinardo, the consultant structural engineer, who was responsible for all the structural work for the whole project, was presented with a unique design situation. She was asked to redesign the steelwork on the fly floors, counterweight flying system and grid, which had originally been conceived by her father Carlo for the 1982 refurbishment.

Another link with that refurbishment was made by John Cormack, of RIM construction, who fabricated all the steelwork. He had previously been connected with Bon Accord Construction, the company which did the same job in 1982. The use of local craftsmen continued when the contract for painting and decoration was awarded to Lawrence Milne & Sons of Ellon.

The total cost for the project, estimated at £7.8 million, was met by the core funders, Aberdeen City Council, the Scottish Arts Council Lottery Fund and Scottish Enterprise.

One incident that occurred during the building works is worthy of mention. Early on a Saturday afternoon, David Steel was in the Front Stalls area with the carpet layers. They were anxious to vacate the building fairly quickly as there was a home game at Pittodrie that day. There were no other workmen in the building. As they were about to leave, footsteps were heard on the fly floor above the stage. Having seen Karen Dinardo's car parked at the rear of the theatre, David assumed that she was checking on progress up on the fly floor. He called to warn her that they were about to lock up the building. No reply – but more footsteps. He called again. No reply. More footsteps. David then had a brilliant idea. He would call her on her mobile. Success! Karen answered. She was at the hairdresser's getting her hair done!

The fly floor above the stage

Perhaps Jake had decided to return to his old haunting ground!

Now in all
its glory

The refurbished auditorium

The foyer, box office and coffee shop

The new gallery foyer

The corporate hospitality suite

The green room

The spacious office

The rehearsal suite

Matcham's, the new restaurant

MATCHAM'S
RESTAURANT / CAFÉ BAR

Frank Matcham
Theatre Architect
1854 - 1920

His Royal Highness, Earl of Wessex, KCVO,
unveiled this bust of Frank Matcham on the
occasion of the re-opening of His Majesty's
Theatre, following it's extension and major
redevelopment, on 8th September 2005.

Sculptor : Gareth Knowles

The bust of Frank Matcham, displayed in the old foyer

The Finale

Looking Towards the Future

Three times in the one-hundred-year life of His Majesty's Theatre, the building has been refurbished to meet the expectations of successive ages. In 1933, it had to meet the challenge of cinema entertainment. In 1982, it had to comply with health and safety regulations. In 2005, the new extension was added to ensure that the theatre was open, welcoming and available for daytime use.

Throughout all these changes, the original brilliant concept by Frank Matcham has remained intact and indeed has been enhanced. His building stands as an architectural gem, an important contributor to Aberdeen's cultural heritage. The new extension does not compete with that – it complements it, giving it new life and fresh vigour. It is an architectural statement in its own right, reflecting contemporary thought and design, but built with the same attention to detail, the same quality of materials and craftsmanship as the original. His Majesty's Theatre is now fit and ready to face an exciting future.

The management have dedicated themselves to continuing to bring the finest touring productions to the city, catering for all tastes and interests. They have promised a new life for the theatre as a catalyst for new writing, reflecting, though not exclusively, the life and culture of our own area. The new educational programme is already providing opportunities for schoolchildren and adults to experience the thrill of theatrical life and an understanding of all the theatrical crafts. The rehearsal suite is already in constant use. The youth theatre is providing a training ground and a melting pot for the star performers of the future. His Majesty's is now open and welcoming. The restaurant and coffee shop are bright and cheerful and popular as a meeting place for friends.

All that is needed for a long and healthy future is for the citizens of Aberdeen and the surrounding area to accept the invitation to enjoy and participate in all that the venue has to offer. The city fathers have invested heavily on their behalf – £250,000 in 1974, £3.5 million in 1982 and £7.8 million in 2005. Since the 1970s, they have supported His Majesty's Theatre as part of their annual expenditure on cultural development. It is therefore appropriate to end this account celebrating the centenary of His Majesty's Theatre by recalling the challenge made by Robert Arthur on that opening night on 3 December 1906:

> Now it remains with the people of Aberdeen to put the copestone of success on what the craftsmen of Aberdeen have builded with such care.

Encore

More Images from the Story of His Majesty's Theatre

George, Edi, Sandy and John –
unsung heroes of *Student Shows*

Workers from James Scott & Sons

Programme from Royal
Gala Show 1978 in aid
of The Prince of Wales'
charities and starring
The Three Degrees

James and Anne Donald pour the drinks at the final party 1980

The exciting new extension, 2005

Theatre logos used over the years

Staff photograph taken to celebrate Walter S. Gilbert's lease of the theatre in 1923

Staff photograph taken in 1986 to celebrate the theatre's 80th birthday

Staff photograph taken in 1996 to celebrate the theatre's 90th birthday

An informal and happy picture of the 2006 staff celebrating the theatre's centenary

His Majesty's Theatre, Perth, Australia

A Postscript

Our Twin in Australia

Only two theatres in the world built during the reign of Edward VII share the title of His Majesty's Theatre. During the celebrations for the centenary of His Majesty's in Perth Australia, Graeme Roberts and Duncan Hendry from His Majesty's, Aberdeen, were honoured guests and exchanged gifts with their hosts.

The twinning ceremony will be finalised in autumn 2006 when the mayor and theatre management from Perth will be the guests at a civic reception in the City of Aberdeen.

The twinning ceremony in Perth

Recommended Reading

Adair, Elizabeth, *North East Folk from Cottage to Castle* (Paul Harris, 1982)

Adams, Norman, *Haunted Neuk* (Tolbooth, 1994)

Devlin, Vivien, *Kings, Queens and People's Palaces* (Polygon, 1991)

Earl, John and Michael Sell, *Guide to British Theatres* 1750–1950 (A. & C. Black, 2000)

Irving, Gordon, *The Good Auld Days* (Jupiter, 1977)

Lewis, Roy Harley, *Theatre Ghosts* (David & Charles, 1988)

Littlejohn, J. H., *The Tivoli Theatre* (Showstoppers, 2000)

Peter, Bruce, *Scotland's Splendid Theatres* (Polygon, 1999)

Watson, Iain, *Harry Gordon* (City of Aberdeen, 1993)

Picture Credits

Index